CRIMINAL JUSTICE, LAW ENFORCEMENT AND CORRECTIONS SERIES

MASS MARKETING AND CONSUMER FRAUD: BACKGROUND, ISSUES AND DATA

CRIMINAL JUSTICE, LAW ENFORCEMENT AND CORRECTIONS SERIES

Gun Ownership and the Second Amendment
Pjeter D. Baldrige
2009. ISBN: 978-1-60692-226-2

Homicide Investigations
Allan B. Smythe
2009. ISBN: 978-1-60692-258-3

Digital Surveillance: Laws, Security and Related Issues
Joseph G. Massingale (Editor)
2009. ISBN: 978-1-60692-312-2

Mass Incarceration and Offender Reentry in the United States
Russell D. Javitze (Editor)
2009. ISBN: 978-1-60692-657-4

Incarceration and the Family: Issues, Effects and Approaches to Successful Reentry
United States Department of Health and Human Services
2009. ISBN: 978-1-60692-933-9

Batterer Intervention: Program Approaches and Criminal Justice Strategies
Kerry Healey, Christine Smith,and Chris O'Sullivan
2009. ISBN: 978-1-60692-934-6

Batterer Intervention: Program Approaches and Criminal Justice Strategies
Kerry Healey, Christine Smith and Chris O'Sullivan
2009. ISBN: 978-1-60876-537-9
(Online Book)

Delinquency: Causes, Reduction and Prevention
Ozan Sahin and Joseph Maier (Editor)
2009. ISBN: 978-1-60741-558-9

Homicide: Trends, Causes and Prevention
Randal B. Toliver and Ulrich R. Coyne (Editors)
2009. ISBN: 978-1-60741-625-8

Violent Crime and Prisons: Population, Health Conditions and Recidivism
Aidan Renshaw and Emelina Suárez (Editors)
2009. ISBN: 978-1-60741-668-5

Policing the Police: Knowledge Management in Law Enforcement
Petter Gottschalk
2009. ISBN: 978-1-60741-765-1

Policing the Police: Knowledge Management in Law Enforcement
Petter Gottschalk
2009. ISBN: 978-1-60876-653-6
(Online Book)

Selective Prosecution in the Federal Criminal Justice System?
Kevin H. Mabe (Editor)
2010. ISBN: 978-1-60692-684-0

Police and Augmented Reality Technology
Matthew D. Blount (Editor)
2010. ISBN: 978-1-60692-206-4

Guidelines for Domestic FBI Operations
Carlo Bianchi (Editor)
2010. ISBN: 978-1-60692-798-4

Revisiting the Social Contract: Community Justice and Public Safety
Kathleen Auerhahn and Caitlin J. McGuire
2010. ISBN: 978-1-60876-446-4

Mass Marketing and Consumer Fraud: Background, Issues and Data
Martin A. Parham (Editor)
2010. ISBN: 978-1-60692-793-9

CRIMINAL JUSTICE, LAW ENFORCEMENT AND CORRECTIONS SERIES

MASS MARKETING AND CONSUMER FRAUD: BACKGROUND, ISSUES AND DATA

MARTIN A. PARHAM
EDITOR

Nova Science Publishers, Inc.
New York

For permission to use material from this book please contact us:
Telephone 631-231-7269; Fax 631-231-8175
Web Site: http://www.novapublishers.com

LIBRARY OF CONGRESS CATALOGING-IN-PUBLICATION DATA

Mass marketing and consumer fraud : background, issues, and data / editor, Martin A. Parham.
p. cm.
Includes index.
ISBN 978-1-60692-793-9 (hardcover)
1. Marketing--United States. 2. Fraud--United States. 3. Consumer protection--Law and legislation--United States. I. Parham, Martin A.
HF5415.1.M377 2009
364.16'3--dc22
2009031710

Published by Nova Science Publishers, Inc. ✦ New York

Contents

PREFACE

This book explores consumer fraud and identity theft as well as telemarketing fraud which is both the oldest, and in some respects, the most persistent form of mass-marketing fraud that Canada and the United States have been actively combating for more than a decade now. Additionally, this book has three main purposes: first, it will describe the principal trends and developments since 2003 in the four major types of crime associated with mass-marketing fraud. Second, it will summarize the present approaches that law enforcement in both countries have adopted since 2003 and third, it will report on recommendations that the subgroup made in 2003 as part of a bi-national action plan to fight this fraud. Additional recommendations are also examined that would address changes in the nature and types of mass-marketing fraud that have emerged since 2003.

Chapter 1 - Between January and December 2007, Consumer Sentinel, the complaint database developed and maintained by the Federal Trade Commission (FTC), received over **800,000** consumer fraud and identity theft complaints. Consumers reported losses from fraud of more than $1.2 billion.

Consumer Sentinel collects information about consumer fraud and identity theft from the FTC and over 125 other organizations and makes it available to law enforcement partners across the nation and throughout the world for use in their investigations. Launched in 1997, the Sentinel database now includes over 4.3 million complaints. Some future data transfers from other organizations will contain complaints from 2007 but have not yet been received. Accordingly, the total number of complaints reflected in this chapter may increase over the course of the next few months. The addition of complaints from other data contributors is also reflected in the totals from previous years than were reported in earlier FTC reports.

Chapter 2 - In April 1997, then-Prime Minister of Canada Jean Chrétien and then-President of the United States Bill Clinton directed the preparation of a joint study examining ways to counter the serious and growing problem of cross-border telemarketing fraud. In November 2007, a binational working group established for that purpose provided a report to the Prime Minister and the President that contains a detailed examination of the problem and a series of recommendations to improve both countries' responses to the problem.[1] Those recommendations included identification of telemarketing fraud as a serious crime; establishment of regional task forces to cooperate across the international border; coordination of strategies to control telemarketing fraud between both countries at agency, regional, and national levels; operation of an ongoing binational working group to provide overall coordination; and other recommendations to address information-gathering, evidence-sharing and mutual legal assistance, extradition, and public education and prevention.[2]

The 1997 Report became a general blueprint for coordinated binational actions against telemarketing fraud. In the ten years since the issuance of the 1997 Report, Canada and the United States have not only carried out all of the recommendations in that Report, but have made even greater strides in combating what is now termed mass-marketing fraud - i.e., fraud schemes that use mass communications methods, such as telemarketing, the Internet, and mass mailing to contact and communicate with large numbers of prospective victims and to obtain funds from victims.

This chapter has three purposes. First, it will describe the principal trends and developments since 2003 in four major types of crime associated with mass-marketing fraud (i.e., telemarketing fraud schemes, Internet fraud schemes, Nigerian fraud[3], and identity theft). Second, it will summarize the principal approaches that law enforcement in both countries have adopted since 2003 to combat mass-marketing fraud more effectively. Third, it will report on recommendations that this Subgroup made in 2003 as part of a binational action plan to combat mass-marketing fraud, and set out additional recommendations that address changes in the nature and types of mass-marketing fraud that have emerged since 2003.

In: Mass Marketing and Consumer Fraud…
Editor: Martin A. Parham
ISBN: 978-1-60692-793-9

Chapter 1

CONSUMER FRAUD AND IDENTITY THEFT COMPLAINT DATA, JANUARY-DECEMBER 2007*

Federal Trade Commission

INTRODUCTION

Between January and December 2007, Consumer Sentinel, the complaint database developed and maintained by the Federal Trade Commission (FTC), received over **800,000** consumer fraud and identity theft complaints. Consumers reported losses from fraud of more than $1.2 billion. The reports in this booklet analyze those complaints.

Consumer Sentinel collects information about consumer fraud and identity theft from the FTC and over 125 other organizations and makes it available to law enforcement partners across the nation and throughout the world for use in their investigations. Launched in 1997, the Sentinel database now includes over 4.3 million complaints. Some future data transfers from other organizations will contain complaints from 2007 but have not yet been received. Accordingly, the total number of complaints reflected in this chapter may increase over the course of the next few months. The addition of complaints from other data contributors is also reflected in the totals from previous years than were reported in earlier FTC reports.

Please note: This chapter is not based on a survey; the complaint figures presented are derived from self-reported and unverified consumer complaints contained in the FTC's database.

For more information about Consumer Sentinel, as well as information about consumer fraud and identity theft, visit the Consumer Sentinel public website at www.consumer.gov/sentinel. If you represent a law enforcement organization, call (877) 7019595 or e-mail sentinel@ftc.gov for membership information.

---

* This is an edited, reformatted and augmented version of a Federal Trade Commission publication dated February 2008.

Australian Competition and Consumer Commission	*Better Business Bureaus*
Department of Defense	*Federal Bureau of Investigation*
Federal Trade Commission	*Internet Crime Complaint Center*
National Association of Attorneys General	*National Consumers League*
Canada's Phonebusters	*Social Security Administration*
U.S. Postal Inspection Service	*U.S. Secret Service*

The Consumer Sentinel Network (For detailed description and data contributors, see Appendices A1 through A3)

EXECUTIVE SUMMARY

- Consumer Sentinel now contains over 4.3 million fraud and identity theft complaints and is accessible to over 1,700 law enforcement agencies – including every state attorney general in the U.S. and consumer protection agencies in 23 nations.
- The FTC received over 800,000 Consumer Sentinel complaints during calendar year 2007 - 32% were identity theft complaints and 68% were related to other types of fraud.

Fraud

- A total of 555,472 of the Consumer Sentinel complaints were fraud-related. Shop-at-Home/Catalog Sales was the leading complaint category with 8% of the overall complaints, followed by Internet Services (5%), Foreign Money Offers (4%), Prizes/Sweepstakes and Lotteries (4%), Computer Equipment and Software (3%), Internet Auctions (3%), Health Care (2%), Travel, Vacations and Timeshare (2%), Advance-Fee Loans and Credit Protection/Repair (2%) Investments (2%), and Magazines and Buyers Clubs (2%).
- Consumers reported fraud losses of over $1.2 billion; the median monetary loss was $349. Eighty-nine percent of the consumers reporting fraud also reported an amount paid.
- The percentage of fraud complaints with wire transfer as the reported payment method continues to increase. Twenty-eight percent of the consumers reported wire transfer as the payment method, an increase of 5 percentage points from calendar year 2006.
- Some 64% of fraud complaints where the company's method of initial contact was reported indicate Internet solicitations - electronic mail at 49% and web at 15%. Fifty-three percent of all fraud complaints reported the method of initial contact.
- The metropolitan areas with the highest per capita rates of reported consumer fraud complaints are Albany-Lebanon, Oregon; Greeley, Colorado; and Napa, California.

Identity Theft

- Credit card fraud (23%) was the most common form of reported identity theft followed by phone or utilities fraud (18%), employment fraud (14%) and bank fraud (13%). Other significant categories of identity theft reported by victims were government documents/benefits fraud (11%) and loan fraud (5%).
- Electronic fund transfer-related identity theft continues to be the most frequently reported type of identity theft bank fraud during calendar year 2007.
- The metropolitan areas with the highest per capita rates of reported identity theft are Napa, California; Madera, California; and Greeley, Colorado.

SENTINEL COMPLAINTS BY CALENDAR YEAR[1]

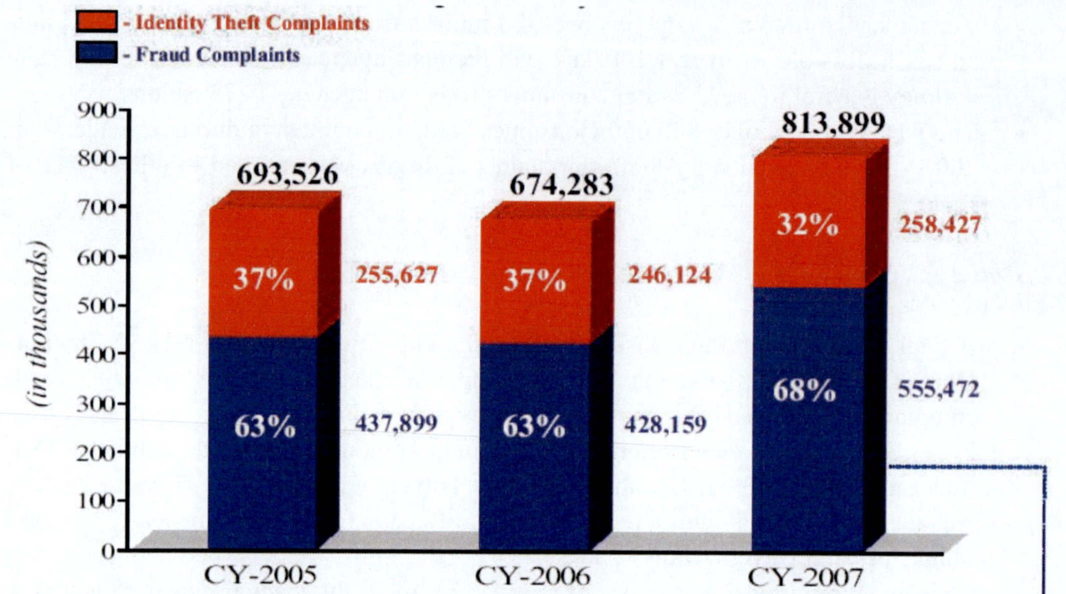

[1] Percentages are based on the total number of Sentinel complaints by calendar year. These figures exclude National Do Not Call Registry complaints.

FRAUD COMPLAINTS BY CALENDAR YEAR[2] (EXCLUDING IDENTITY THEFT)

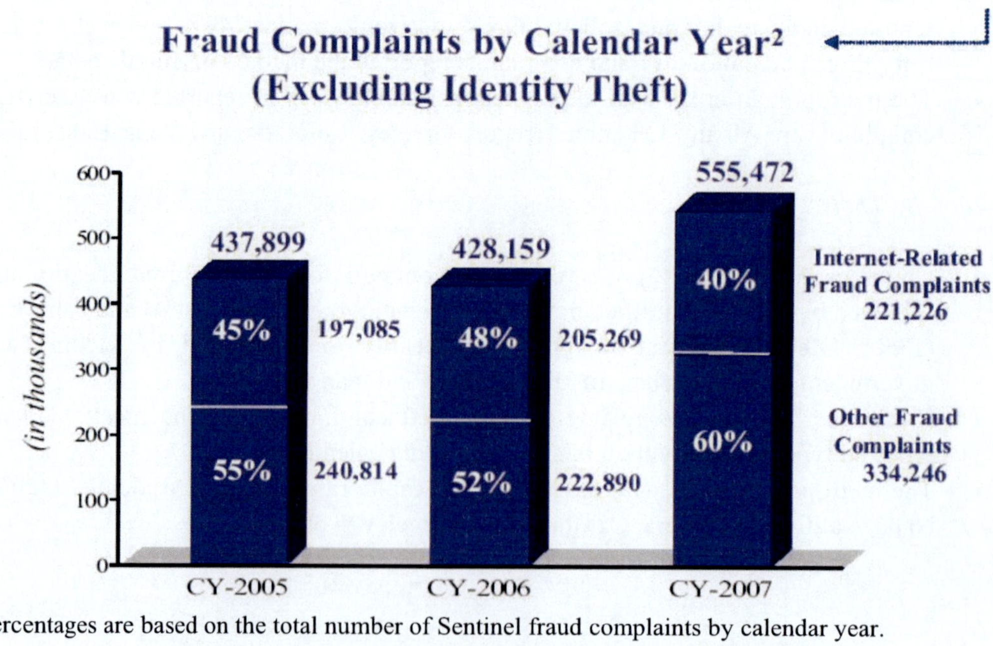

[2] Percentages are based on the total number of Sentinel fraud complaints by calendar year.

SENTINEL TOP COMPLAINT CATEGORIES[1]
JANUARY 1 – DECEMBER 31, 2007

Rank	Top Categories	Complaints	Percentage[1]
1	Identity Theft	258,427	32%
2	Shop-at-Home/Catalog Sales	62,811	8%
3	Internet Services[2]	42,266	5%
4	Foreign Money Offers	32,868	4%
5	Prizes/Sweepstakes and Lotteries	32,162	4%
6	Computer Equipment and Software[2]	27,036	3%
7	Internet Auctions	24,376	3%
8	Health Care	16,097	2%
9	Travel, Vacations and Timeshare	14,903	2%
10	Advance-Fee Loans and Credit Protection/Repair	14,342	2%
11	Investments	13,705	2%
12	Magazines and Buyers Clubs	12,970	2%
13	Business Opps and Work-at-Home Plans	11,362	1%
14	Real Estate (Not Timeshares)	9,475	1%
15	Office Supplies and Services	9,211	1%
16	Telephone Services	8,155	1%
17	Employ Agencies/Job Counsel/Overseas Work	5,932	1%
18	Debt Management/Credit Counseling	3,442	<1%
19	Multi-Level Mktg/Pyramids/Chain Letters	3,092	<1%
20	Charitable Solicitations	1,843	<1%

[1] Percentages are based on the total number of Sentinel complaints (813,899) received by the FTC between January 1 and December 31, 2007. Twenty-five percent (200,136) of the Sentinel complaints received by the FTC did not contain specific product service codes. For Sentinel category descriptions, see Appendix B.

[2] In previous reports, complaints for "Internet Services" and "Computer Equipment and Software" were reported under a combined category.

TOTAL NUMBER OF FRAUD COMPLAINTS & AMOUNT PAID
CALENDAR YEARS 2005 THROUGH 2007

CY	Total No. of Complaints	Complaints Reporting Amount Paid	Percentage of Complaints Reporting Amount Paid	Amount Paid Reported	Average Amount Paid[1]	Median Amount Paid[2]
2005	437,899	285,184	65%	$683,018,044	$2,395	$349
2006	428,159	364,454	85%	$1,187,174,644	$3,257	$500
2007	555,472	493,530	89%	$1,237,434,851	$2,507	$349

[1] Average is based on the total number of consumers who reported amount paid for each calendar year: CY-2005 = 285,184; CY-2006 = 364,454 ; and CY-2007 = 493,530. Two hundred forty-five consumers reported an amount paid of $1 million or more during CY-2007; 49 and 184 consumers for CY-2005 and CY-2006, respectively.

[2] Median is the middle number in a set of numbers so that half the numbers have values that are greater than the median and half have values that are less. Calculation of the median excludes complaints with amount paid reported as $0.

Distribution of Fraud Complaints by Reported Amount Paid Calendar Years 2005 through 2007

Amount Paid	*CY - 2005* Complaints	*CY - 2005* Percentages[3]	*CY - 2006* Complaints	*CY - 2006* Percentages[3]	*CY - 2007* Complaints	*CY - 2007* Percentages[3]
$0	91,037	32%	154,239	42%	270,041	55%
$1 - 25	17,044	6%	15,279	4%	15,746	3%
$26 - 50	17,611	6%	15,719	4%	20,071	4%
$51 - 75	9,806	3%	9,056	2%	11,711	2%
$76 - 100	9,432	3%	9,223	3%	12,405	3%
$101 - 250	30,367	11%	28,586	8%	38,425	8%
$251 - 500	27,440	10%	28,377	8%	31,765	6%
$501 - 1,000	23,424	8%	29,585	8%	28,145	6%
$1,001 - 5,000	45,110	16%	58,240	16%	49,962	10%
More than $5,000	13,913	5%	16,150	4%	15,259	3%

[3] Percentages are based on the total number of consumers who reported amount paid for each calendar year: CY-2005 = 285,184; CY-2006 = 364,454; and CY-2007 = 493,530.

Methods of Payment Reported by Consumers[1] January 1 - December 31, 2007

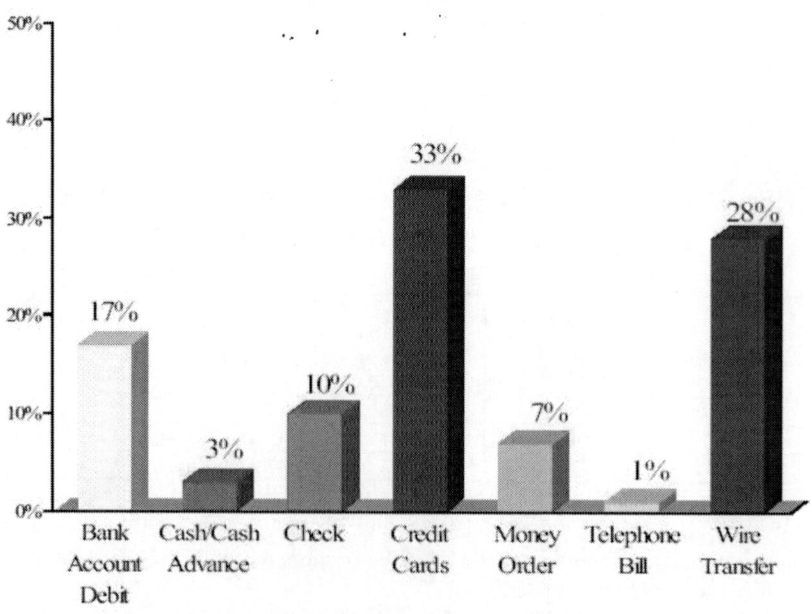

Methods of Payment Reported by Consumers
Calendar Years 2005 through 2007

		CY - 2005			*CY - 2006*			*CY - 2007*	
Payment Method	**Complaints**	**Percentages**[1]	**Amount Paid**	**Complaints**	**Percentages**[1]	**Amount Paid**	**Complaints**	**Percentages**[1]	**Amount Paid**
Bank Account Debit	14,802	23%	$ 26,448,169	13,156	20%	$ 37,712,964	11,726	17%	$ 29,371,619
Cash/Cash Advance	2,383	4%	$ 17,210,216	2,444	4%	$ 13,245,360	2,334	3%	$ 18,187,539
Check	10,440	16%	$ 75,252,950	8,628	13%	$ 96,464,400	6,757	10%	$ 80,035,706
Credit Cards	19,371	30%	$ 36,735,021	20,475	30%	$ 40,677,855	22,324	33%	$ 49,770,123
Money Order	7,200	11%	$ 12,538,520	5,913	9%	$ 20,357,643	4,596	7%	$ 31,071,393
Telephone Bill	1,175	2%	$ 491,499	1,267	2%	$ 418,295	974	1%	$ 295,724
Wire Transfer	9,485	15%	$ 86,558,141	15,460	23%	$ 149,640,338	18,484	28%	$ 130,958,802
Total Reporting Payment Method	*64,856*			*67,343*			*67,195*		

[1] Percentages are based on the total number of fraud complaints for each calendar year where consumers reported the method of payment: CY-2005 = 64,856; CY-2006 = 67,343; and CY-2007 = 67,195. 12% of the consumers reported this information during CY-2007, 15% and 16% for CY-2005 and CY-2006, respectively.

COMPANY'S METHOD OF CONTACTING CONSUMERS[1]
JANUARY 1 - DECEMBER 31, 2007

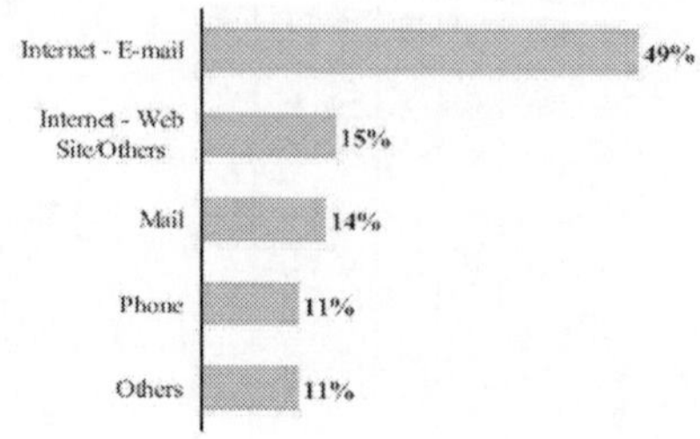

COMPANY'S METHOD OF CONTACTING CONSUMERS
CALENDAR YEARS 2005 THROUGH 2007

Contact Method	*CY - 2005*		*CY - 2006*		*CY - 2007*	
	Complaints	Percentages[1]	Complaints	Percentages[1]	Complaints	Percentages[1]
Internet - E-mail	111,480	34%	138,144	45%	142,445	49%
Internet - Web Site/Others	64,060	20%	46,696	15%	44,244	15%
Mail	59,761	18%	50,350	16%	40,542	14%
Phone	53,536	17%	39,399	13%	31,769	11%
Others	34,853	11%	31,746	10%	32,780	11%
Total Reporting Contact Method	*323,690*		*306,335*		*291,780*	

[1] Percentages are based on the total number of fraud complaints for each calendar year where company's method of initial contact was reported by consumers: CY-2005 = 323,690; CY-2006 = 306,335; and CY-2007 = 291,780. 53% of consumers reported this information during CY-2007, 74% and 72% for CY-2005 and CY-2006, respectively.

FRAUD COMPLAINTS BY CONSUMER AGE[1]
JANUARY 1 - DECEMBER 31, 2007

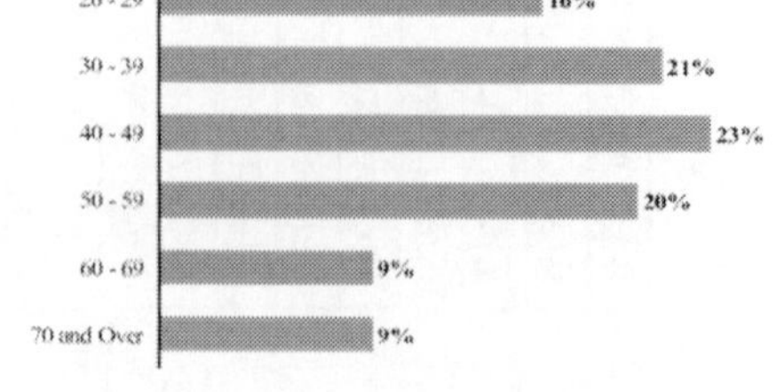

FRAUD COMPLAINTS BY CONSUMER AGE CALENDAR YEARS 2005 THROUGH 2007

Consumer Age Range	*CY - 2005*		*CY - 2006*		*CY - 2007*	
	Complaints	**Percentages**[1]	**Complaints**	**Percentages**[1]	**Complaints**	**Percentages**[1]
19 and Under	8,025	3%	2,657	2%	2,081	2%
20-29	65,342	20%	23,361	16%	20,538	16%
30-39	72,335	23%	29,112	21%	26,501	21%
40-49	74,397	23%	33,037	23%	29,157	23%
50-59	59,108	18%	28,879	20%	25,725	20%
60-69	23,783	7%	11,728	8%	11,071	9%
70 and Over	16,969	5%	12,905	9%	11,586	9%
Total Reporting Age	*319,959*		*141,679*		*126,659*	

[1] Percentages are based on the total number of consumers reporting their age in fraud complaints for each calendar year: CY-2005 = 319,959; CY-2006 = 141,679; and CY-2007 = 126,659. 23% of consumers reported this information during CY-2007, 73% and 33% for CY-2005 and CY-2006, respectively.

Definition of "Internet-related": A fraud complaint is "Internet-related" if it concerns an Internet product or service, the company initially contacts the consumer via the Internet, or the consumer responds via the Internet.

TOTAL NUMBER OF INTERNET-RELATED FRAUD COMPLAINTS & AMOUNT PAID CALENDAR YEARS 2005 THROUGH 2007

CY	Total No. of Complaints	Complaints Reporting Amount Paid	Percentage of Complaints Reporting Amount Paid	Amount Paid Reported	Average Amount Paid[1]	Median Amount Paid[2]
2005	197,085	160,573	81%	$336,345,604	$2,095	$342
2006	205,269	177,245	86%	$590,494,777	$3,332	$500
2007	221,226	192,558	87%	$525,743,643	$2,730	$395

[1] Average is based on the total number of consumers who reported amount paid for each calendar year: CY-2005 = 160,573; CY-2006 = 177,245; and CY-2007= 192,558. Eighty-six consumers reported an amount paid of $1 million or more during CY-2007; 24 and 85 consumers for CY-2005 and CY-2006, respectively.

[2] Median is the middle number in a set of numbers so that half the numbers have values that are greater than the median and half have values that are less. Calculation of the median excludes complaints with amount paid reported as $0.

Distribution of Internet-Related Fraud Complaints by Reported Amount Paid Calendar Years 2005 through 2007

Amount Paid	CY - 2005		CY - 2006		CY - 2007	
	Complaints	Percentages[3]	Complaints	Percentages[3]	Complaints	Percentages[3]
$0	35,957	22%	75,589	43%	98,666	51%
$1 - 25	10,294	6%	6,836	4%	6,490	3%
$26 - 50	11,319	7%	7,130	4%	7,596	4%
$51 - 75	6,840	4%	4,479	3%	4,630	2%
$76 - 100	6,303	4%	4,564	3%	4,776	2%
$101 - 250	20,234	13%	14,163	8%	15,912	8%
$251 - 500	17,597	11%	14,150	8%	12,838	7%
$501 - 1,000	16,491	10%	15,740	9%	12,175	6%
$1,001 - 5,000	28,191	18%	26,903	15%	22,458	12%
More than $5,000	7,347	5%	7,691	4%	7,017	4%

[3] Percentages are based on the total number of consumers who reported amount paid for each calendar year: CY-2005 = 160,573; CY-2006 = 177,245; and CY-2007 = 192,558.

Definition of "Internet-related": A fraud complaint is "Internet-related" if it concerns an Internet product or service, the company initially contacts the consumer via the Internet, or the consumer responds via the Internet.

Methods of Payment Reported by Consumers For Internet-Related Fraud Complaints[1] January 1 - December 31, 2007

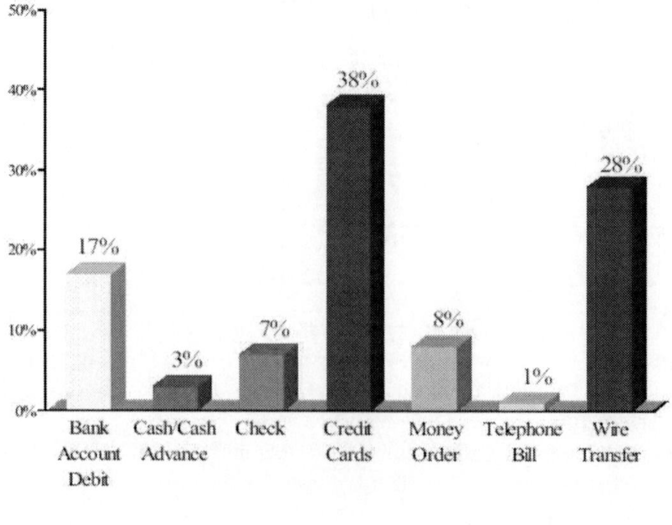

Methods of Payment Reported by Consumers For Internet-Related Fraud Complaints Calendar Years 2005 through 2007

		CY - 2005			*CY - 2006*			*CY - 2007*	
Payment Method	**Complaints**	**Percentages[1]**	**Amount Paid**	**Complaints**	**Percentages[1]**	**Amount Paid**	**Complaints**	**Percentages[1]**	**Amount Paid**
Bank Account Debit	6,153	19%	$ 11,181,001	6,643	18%	$ 21,792,498	6,653	17%	$ 13,751,585
Cash/Cash Advance	1,039	3%	$ 11,164,636	1,169	3%	$ 7,648,293	1,216	3%	$ 7,943,260
Check	3,437	10%	$ 21,804,907	2,850	8%	$ 60,119,725	2,577	7%	$ 17,906,180
Credit Cards	12,208	37%	$ 19,004,962	12,927	35%	$ 24,736,839	14,822	38%	$ 30,681,611
Money Order	3,997	12%	$ 7,839,943	3,660	10%	$ 16,661,396	2,962	8%	$ 25,663,620
Telephone Bill	424	1%	$ 96,364	429	1%	$ 259,659	298	1%	$ 112,452
Wire Transfer	5,557	17%	$ 41,786,350	8,769	24%	$ 91,623,738	10,857	28%	$ 76,670,821
Total Reporting Payment Method	*32,815*			*36,447*			*39,385*		

[1]Percentages are based on the total number of Internet-related fraud complaints for each calendar year where consumers reported the method of payment: CY-2005 = 32,815; CY-2006 = 36,447; and CY-2007 = 39,385. 18% of the consumers reported this information during CY-2007, 17% and 18% for CY-2005 and CY-2006, respectively.

Definition of "Internet-related": A fraud complaint is "Internet-related" if: it concerns an Internet product or service, the company initially contacts the consumer via the Internet, or the consumer responds via the Internet.

INTERNET-RELATED FRAUD COMPLAINTS BY CONSUMER AGE[1] JANUARY 1 - DECEMBER 31, 2007

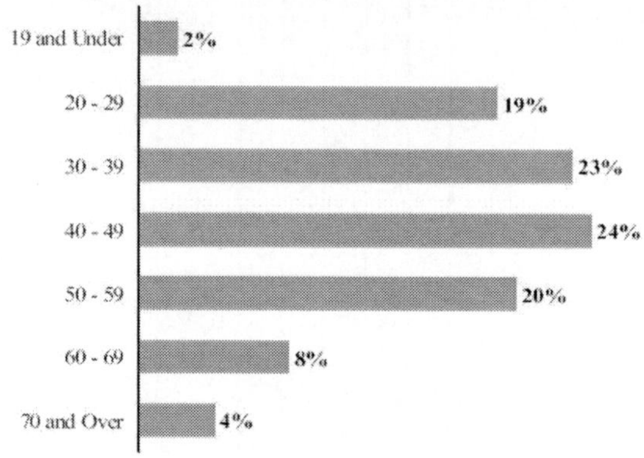

INTERNET-RELATED FRAUD COMPLAINTS BY CONSUMER AGE CALENDAR YEARS 2005 THROUGH 2007

Consumer Age Range	*CY - 2005*		*CY - 2006*		*CY - 2007*	
	Complaints	Percentages[1]	Complaints	Percentages[1]	Complaints	Percentages[1]
19 and Under	5,501	3%	1,495	2%	1,246	2%
20-29	40,041	25%	11,899	19%	11,225	19%
30-39	39,803	25%	14,420	24%	13,889	23%
40-49	37,585	24%	14,954	24%	14,362	24%
50-59	25,840	16%	12,052	20%	11,798	20%
60-69	8,468	5%	4,544	7%	4,638	8%
70 and Over	2,590	2%	1,802	3%	2,366	4%
Total Reporting Age	*159,828*		*61,166*		*59,524*	

[1] Percentages are based on the total number of consumers reporting their age in Internet-related fraud complaints for each calendar year: CY-2005 = 159,828; CY-2006 = 61,166; and CY-2007 = 59,524. 27% of consumers reported this information during CY-2007, 81% and 30% for CY-2005 and CY-2006, respectively.

HOW VICTIMS' INFORMATION IS MISUSED[1]
CALENDAR YEARS 2005 THROUGH 2007

Credit Card Fraud			
	Percentages	**Percentages**	**Percentages**
Theft Subtype	CY-2005	CY-2006	CY-2007
New Accounts	15.6%	15.2%	14.2%
Existing Account	11.4%	10.7%	9.4%
Unspecified	0.2%	0.2%	0.2%
Total	**26%**	**25%**	**23%**

Phone or Utilities Fraud			
	Percentages	**Percentages**	**Percentages**
Theft Subtype	CY-2005	CY-2006	CY-2007
Telephone - New Accounts	5.5%	4.4%	7.3%
Wireless - New Accounts	9.0%	7.2%	6.5%
Utilities - New Accounts	5.2%	5.8%	5.2%
Unauthorized Charges to Existing Accounts	0.7%	0.7%	0.5%
Unspecified	0.4%	0.5%	0.5%
Total	**18%**	**17%**	**18%**

Employment-Related Fraud			
	Percentages	**Percentages**	**Percentages**
Theft Subtype	CY-2005	CY-2006	CY-2007
Employment-Related Fraud	**12%**	**14%**	**14%**

Bank Fraud[2]			
	Percentages	**Percentages**	**Percentages**
Theft Subtype	CY-2005	CY-2006	CY-2007
Electronic Fund Transfer	8.0%	8.0%	7.0%
Existing Accounts	7.5%	5.8%	4.0%
New Accounts	3.3%	3.1%	3.1%
Unspecified	0.1%	0.1%	0.1%
Total	**18%**	**16%**	**13%**

Loan Fraud			
	Percentages	**Percentages**	**Percentages**
Theft Subtype	CY-2005	CY-2006	CY-2007
Business / Personal / Student Loan	2.6%	2.5%	2.3%
Auto Loan / Lease	1.8%	1.7%	1.4%
Real Estate Loan	1.2%	1.3%	1.3%
Unspecified	0.2%	0.2%	0.3%
Total	**5%**	**5%**	**5%**

Other Identity Theft			
	Percentages	**Percentages**	**Percentages**
Theft Subtype	CY-2005	CY-2006	CY-2007
Uncertain[3]	–	12.0%	11.6%
Miscellaneous[3]	–	4.6%	7.4%
Evading the Law	2.2%	2.1%	1.8%
Medical	1.9%	2.0%	1.6%
Internet / Email	2.0%	2.2%	1.4%
Apartment or House Rented	0.9%	0.9%	0.6%
Insurance	0.4%	0.4%	0.3%
Property Rental Fraud	0.3%	0.3%	0.3%
Securities / Other Investments	0.2%	0.2%	0.3%
Child Support	0.2%	0.2%	0.2%
Bankruptcy	0.3%	0.2%	0.2%
Magazines	0.2%	0.2%	0.2%
Other[3]	17.4%	–	–
Sum:	**25%**	**24%**	**25%**

Attempted Identity Theft			
	Percentages	**Percentages**	**Percentages**
Theft Subtype	CY-2005	CY-2006	CY-2007
Attempted Identity Theft	**6%**	**6%**	**5%**

Government Documents or Benefits Fraud			
	Percentages	**Percentages**	**Percentages**
Theft Subtype	CY-2005	CY-2006	CY-2007
Fraudulent Tax Return Filed	4.8%	6.3%	8.0%
Government Benefits Applied For / Received	1.5%	1.3%	1.4%
Driver's License Issued / Forged	1.8%	1.5%	0.9%
Other Government Documents Issued / Forged[4]	0.6%	0.9%	0.7%
Social Security Card Issued / Forged[4]	0.2%	–	–
Unspecified	<0.1%	<0.1%	<0.1%
Total	**9%**	**10%**	**11%**

[1] Percentages are based on the total number of complaints in the Identity Theft Data Clearinghouse for each calendar year: CY-2005 = 255,627; CY-2006 = 246,124; and CY-2007 = 258,427. Note that 16% of identity theft complaints include more than one type of identity theft in CY-2007, 20% in CY-2005 and 18% in CY-2006.

[2] Includes fraud involving checking and savings accounts and electronic fund transfers.

[3] Theft subtype "Other" was replaced by theft subtypes "Miscellaneous" and "Uncertain" in CY-2006.

[4] Theft subtype "Social Security Card Issued/Forged" was combined with theft subtype "Other Government Documents Issued/Forged" in CY-2006.

LAW ENFORCEMENT CONTACT[1]
JANUARY 1 – DECEMBER 31, 2007

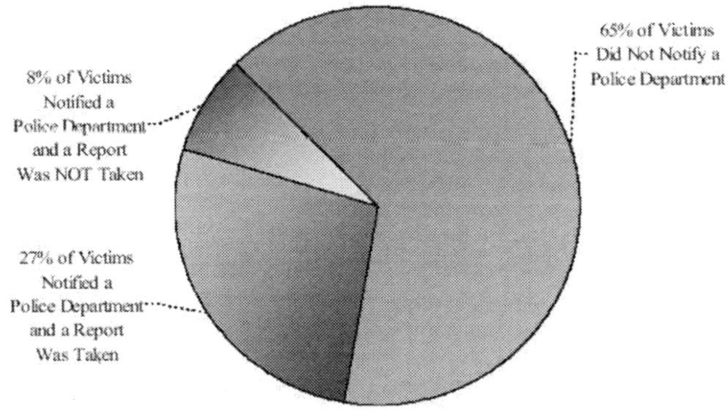

1 Percentages are based on the total number of identity theft complaints where victims indicated whether they had notified a police department (242,341). 99% of the identity theft victims who contacted the FTC directly reported law enforcement contact information. Less than one percent of victims who notified the FTC that they had contacted a police department did not indicate if a report was taken.

LAW ENFORCEMENT CONTACT CALENDAR YEARS 2005 THROUGH 2007

If the victim notified a police department, was a report taken?	CY-2005		CY-2006		CY-2007	
	Complaints	Percentages[2]	Complaints	Percentages[2]	Complaints	Percentages[2]
Yes	74,704	30%	69,072	30%	64,934	27%
No	21,328	9%	18,520	8%	18,634	8%
Not Reported	1,202	<1%	1,070	<1%	238	<1%
Total Who Notified a Police Department	*97,234*	*40%*	*88,662*	*38%*	*83,806*	*35%*
Total Who Did Not Notify a Police Department	*148,752*	*60%*	*144,943*	*62%*	*158,535*	*65%*
Total Reporting Law Enforcement Contact Information	245,986		233,605		242,341	

2 Percentages are based on the total number of identity theft complaints where victims indicated whether they had notified a police department: CY-2005 = 245,986; CY-2006 = 233,605; and CY-2007 = 242,341. 99% of identity theft victims who contacted the FTC directly reported law enforcement contact information in CY-2007, 98% in both CY-2005 and CY-2006.

Identity Theft Complaints by Victim Age[1]
January 1 – December 31, 2007

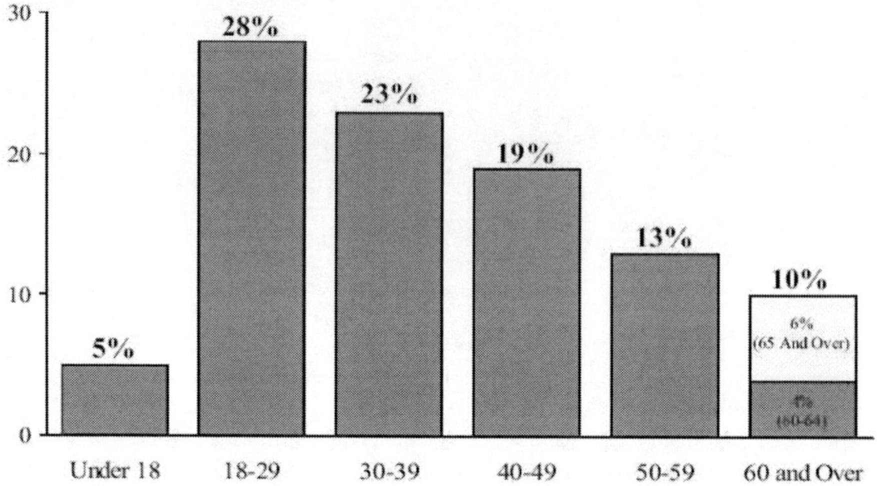

[1] Percentages are based on the total number of identity theft complaints where victims reported their age (231,576). 95% of the victims who contacted the FTC directly reported their age.

Identity Theft Complaints by Victim Age
Calendar Years 2005 through 2007

Consumer Age Range	CY-2005		CY-2006		CY-2007	
	Complaints	Percentages[2]	Complaints	Percentages[2]	Complaints	Percentages[2]
Under 18	11,601	5%	10,838	5%	11,769	5%
18 - 29	70,274	29%	65,757	29%	65,695	28%
30 - 39	56,527	24%	52,631	23%	54,208	23%
40 - 49	47,611	20%	44,721	20%	44,873	19%
50 - 59	30,313	13%	29,383	13%	30,927	13%
60 and Over	23,035	9%	22,305	10%	24,104	10%
60 - 64	8,132	3%	7,988	4%	8,900	4%
65+	14,903	6%	14,317	6%	15,204	6%
Total Reporting Age	*239,361*		*225,635*		*231,576*	

[2] Percentages are based on the total number of identity theft complaints where victims reported their age: CY-2005 = 239,361; CY-2006 = 225,635; and CY-2007 = 231,576. 95% of the victims who contacted the FTC directly reported their age in CY-2007, 95% in CY-2005 and 94% in CY-2006.

LARGEST METROPOLITAN AREAS RANKING FOR FRAUD CONSUMER COMPLAINTS[1] JANUARY 1 – DECEMBER 31, 2007

Rank	Metropolitan Area	Complaints	Complaints Per 100,000 Population
1	Albany-Lebanon, OR Micropolitan Statistical Area	642	575.8
2	Greeley, CO Metropolitan Statistical Area	1,359	573.8
3	Napa, CA Metropolitan Statistical Area	703	526.5
4	Punta Gorda, FL Metropolitan Statistical Area	790	511.5
5	Allegan, MI Micropolitan Statistical Area	522	459.9
6	Roseburg, OR Micropolitan Statistical Area	481	457.6
7	Dunn, NC Micropolitan Statistical Area	472	444.1
8	Willimantic, CT Micropolitan Statistical Area	518	443.2
9	Concord, NH Micropolitan Statistical Area	642	433.5
10	Gainesville, GA Metropolitan Statistical Area	740	427.1
11	Thomasville-Lexington, NC Micropolitan Statistical Area	667	426.9
12	Boulder, CO Metropolitan Statistical Area	1,197	424.0
13	Monroe, MI Metropolitan Statistical Area	652	420.6
14	Prescott, AZ Metropolitan Statistical Area	859	413.0
15	Gettysburg, PA Micropolitan Statistical Area	415	410.5
16	Mount Vernon-Anacortes, WA Metropolitan Statistical Area	472	408.0
17	Michigan City-La Porte, IN Metropolitan Statistical Area	448	405.5
18	Santa Cruz-Watsonville, CA Metropolitan Statistical Area	1,011	404.9
19	New Bern, NC Micropolitan Statistical Area	458	388.6
20	Salisbury, NC Micropolitan Statistical Area	523	383.8
21	Durham, NC Metropolitan Statistical Area	1,780	383.3
22	Olympia, WA Metropolitan Statistical Area	895	381.4
23	Whitewater, WI Micropolitan Statistical Area	380	376.2
24	Niles-Benton Harbor, MI Metropolitan Statistical Area	606	374.8
25	Statesville-Mooresville, NC Micropolitan Statistical Area	544	372.1
26	Torrington, CT Micropolitan Statistical Area	698	367.1
27	East Stroudsburg, PA Micropolitan Statistical Area	602	363.3
28	Yuba City, CA Metropolitan Statistical Area	586	362.2
29	Racine, WI Metropolitan Statistical Area	710	362.1
30	Springfield, OH Metropolitan Statistical Area	513	361.6
31	Colorado Springs, CO Metropolitan Statistical Area	2,166	361.5
32	Sierra Vista-Douglas, AZ Micropolitan Statistical Area	461	360.8
33	Madera, CA Metropolitan Statistical Area	527	360.1
34	Flagstaff, AZ Metropolitan Statistical Area	448	358.5
35	Ann Arbor, MI Metropolitan Statistical Area	1,230	357.5
36	Hanford-Corcoran, CA Metropolitan Statistical Area	519	355.1
37	Lebanon, PA Metropolitan Statistical Area	449	353.9
38	Fort Collins-Loveland, CO Metropolitan Statistical Area	976	353.3

(Continued)

Rank	Metropolitan Area	Complaints	Complaints Per 100,000 Population
39	Lake Havasu City-Kingman, AZ Micropolitan Statistical Area	676	350.2
40	Chambersburg, PA Micropolitan Statistical Area	485	346.5
41	Fort Walton Beach-Crestview-Destin, FL Metropolitan Statistical Area	622	345.0
42	Wausau, WI Metropolitan Statistical Area	449	344.8
43	Vallejo-Fairfield, CA Metropolitan Statistical Area	1,395	338.9
44	Winchester, VA-WV Metropolitan Statistical Area	402	338.0
45	Bellingham, WA Metropolitan Statistical Area	628	337.7
46	Pottsville, PA Micropolitan Statistical Area	486	329.7
47	Reno-Sparks, NV Metropolitan Statistical Area	1,310	327.0
48	Coeur d'Alene, ID Metropolitan Statistical Area	430	327.0
49	Manchester-Nashua, NH Metropolitan Statistical Area	1,311	325.5
50	Appleton, WI Metropolitan Statistical Area	707	325.3

[1] Ranking is based on the number of fraud complaints per 100,000 inhabitants for each Metropolitan Area. This chart illustrates the top 50 Metropolitan Areas (Metropolitan and Micropolitan Statistical Areas) with a population of one hundred thousand or more. See fraud figures for all Metropolitan Areas with a population of 100,000 or more in Appendix C1. Metropolitan Areas presented here are those defined by the Office of Management and Budget as of December 2005 and the population estimates are based on the 2006 U.S. Census table CBSA-EST2006-01.

LARGEST METROPOLITAN AREAS RANKING FOR IDENTITY THEFT CONSUMER COMPLAINTS[1] JANUARY 1 – DECEMBER 31, 2007

Rank	Metropolitan Area	Complaints	Complaints Per 100,000 Population
1	Napa, CA Metropolitan Statistical Area	404	302.6
2	Madera, CA Metropolitan Statistical Area	410	280.2
3	Greeley, CO Metropolitan Statistical Area	540	228.0
4	Brownsville-Harlingen, TX Metropolitan Statistical Area	876	225.9
5	McAllen-Edinburg-Mission, TX Metropolitan Statistical Area	1,563	223.1
6	Vallejo-Fairfield, CA Metropolitan Statistical Area	898	218.1
7	Hanford-Corcoran, CA Metropolitan Statistical Area	314	214.8
8	Dunn, NC Micropolitan Statistical Area	223	209.8
9	Flagstaff, AZ Metropolitan Statistical Area	261	208.9
10	Thomasville-Lexington, NC Micropolitan Statistical Area	322	206.1
11	Yuba City, CA Metropolitan Statistical Area	318	196.5
12	Laredo, TX Metropolitan Statistical Area	454	196.1
13	Lake Havasu City-Kingman, AZ Micropolitan Statistical Area	360	186.5

(Continued)

Rank	Metropolitan Area	Complaints	Complaints Per 100,000 Population
14	Bakersfield, CA Metropolitan Statistical Area	1,436	184.1
15	Yuma, AZ Metropolitan Statistical Area	336	179.1
16	Gainesville, GA Metropolitan Statistical Area	307	177.2
17	Prescott, AZ Metropolitan Statistical Area	366	175.9
18	Monroe, MI Metropolitan Statistical Area	258	166.4
19	Albany-Lebanon, OR Micropolitan Statistical Area	183	164.1
20	Sierra Vista-Douglas, AZ Micropolitan Statistical Area	209	163.6
21	Stockton, CA Metropolitan Statistical Area	1,096	162.8
22	Merced, CA Metropolitan Statistical Area	397	161.6
23	Salisbury, NC Micropolitan Statistical Area	218	160.0
24	Macon, GA Metropolitan Statistical Area	362	157.9
25	Las Cruces, NM Metropolitan Statistical Area	305	157.3
26	Punta Gorda, FL Metropolitan Statistical Area	239	154.8
27	Oxnard-Thousand Oaks-Ventura, CA Metropolitan Statistical Area	1,231	153.9
28	Santa Cruz-Watsonville, CA Metropolitan Statistical Area	383	153.4
29	Phoenix-Mesa-Scottsdale, AZ Metropolitan Statistical Area	6,165	152.6
30	Fresno, CA Metropolitan Statistical Area	1,358	152.3
31	Miami-Fort Lauderdale-Miami Beach, FL Metropolitan Statistical Area	8,317	152.2
32	Montgomery, AL Metropolitan Statistical Area	547	151.2
33	Riverside-San Bernardino-Ontario, CA Metropolitan Statistical Area	6,084	151.1
34	Tucson, AZ Metropolitan Statistical Area	1,422	150.3
35	Hammond, LA Micropolitan Statistical Area	169	149.4
36	Modesto, CA Metropolitan Statistical Area	749	146.2
37	South Bend-Mishawaka, IN-MI Metropolitan Statistical Area	463	145.6
38	Durham, NC Metropolitan Statistical Area	675	145.4
39	Los Angeles-Long Beach-Santa Ana, CA Metropolitan Statistical Area	18,761	144.9
40	El Centro, CA Metropolitan Statistical Area	230	143.5
41	Sebastian-Vero Beach, FL Metropolitan Statistical Area	186	143.0
42	Statesville-Mooresville, NC Micropolitan Statistical Area	209	142.9
43	Visalia-Porterville, CA Metropolitan Statistical Area	595	141.7
44	Ann Arbor, MI Metropolitan Statistical Area	487	141.6
45	Willimantic, CT Micropolitan Statistical Area	165	141.2
46	Mount Vernon-Anacortes, WA Metropolitan Statistical Area	162	140.0
47	Lakeland, FL Metropolitan Statistical Area	784	139.6
48	Pascagoula, MS Metropolitan Statistical Area	211	138.4
49	Dothan, AL Metropolitan Statistical Area	190	137.4
50	Torrington, CT Micropolitan Statistical Area	261	137.3

[1] Ranking is based on the number of identity theft complaints per 100,000 inhabitants for each Metropolitan Area. This chart illustrates the top 50 Metropolitan Areas (Metropolitan and Micropolitan Statistical Areas) with a population of one hundred thousand or more. See identity theft figures for all Metropolitan Areas with a population of 100,000 or more in Appendix C2. Metropolitan Areas presented here are those defined by the Office of Management and Budget as of December 2005 and the population estimates are based on the 2006 U.S. Census table CBSA-EST2006-01.

FRAUD COMPLAINTS BY CONSUMER STATE				IDENTITY THEFT VICTIMS BY STATE			
January 1 - December 31, 2007							
Rank	Consumer State	Complaints Per 100,000 Population	Complaints	Rank	Victim State	Complaints Per 100,000 Population	Complaints
1	Colorado	233.8	11,364	1	Arizona	137.1	8,688
2	Washington	230.6	14,918	2	California	120.1	43,892
3	Missouri	219.7	12,912	3	Nevada	114.2	2,930
4	Arizona	219.3	13,903	4	Texas	107.9	25,796
5	Alaska	209.5	1,432	5	Florida	105.6	19,270
6	Maryland	209.0	11,745	6	New York	100.1	19,319
7	Oregon	205.6	7,704	7	Georgia	91.6	8,744
8	New Hampshire	205.3	2,702	8	Colorado	89.0	4,328
9	Nevada	200.3	5,138	9	New Mexico	87.5	1,723
10	Hawaii	196.4	2,520	10	Maryland	85.8	4,821
11	Utah	193.2	5,110	11	Illinois	80.2	10,304
12	Virginia	191.0	14,733	12	New Jersey	79.0	6,864
13	Florida	181.0	33,027	13	Washington	76.4	4,942
14	Minnesota	180.6	9,388	14	Pennsylvania	72.5	9,016
15	Wisconsin	175.9	9,852	15	Michigan	70.3	7,079
16	Idaho	170.9	2,563	16	Delaware	69.7	603
17	Wyoming	169.1	884	17	Alabama	69.6	3,221
18	Illinois	168.1	21,602	18	Virginia	69.0	5,319
19	California	168.0	61,409	19	Connecticut	68.8	2,409
20	New Jersey	167.4	14,542	20	Oregon	68.1	2,552
21	Georgia	167.0	15,936	21	Missouri	67.4	3,962
22	Ohio	165.4	18,964	22	North Carolina	67.0	6,069
23	Indiana	164.0	10,405	23	Massachusetts	66.5	4,292
24	North Carolina	163.8	14,846	24	Tennessee	64.7	3986
25	Tennessee	161.1	9,920	25	Oklahoma	63.9	2,312
26	Maine	160.3	2,111	26	Indiana	63.4	4,026
27	Nebraska	159.5	2,831	27	Ohio	62.6	7,178
28	Montana	156.2	1,496	28	Louisiana	62.3	2,674
29	Delaware	155.1	1,341	29	Kansas	61.0	1,694
30	Pennsylvania	154.4	19,197	30	South Carolina	60.6	2,670
31	Texas	152.1	36,367	31	Utah	57.8	1,529
32	Massachusetts	151.4	9,766	32	Mississippi	57.3	1,673
33	Connecticut	150.3	5,264	33	Arkansas	56.5	1,601
34	Michigan	146.7	14,780	34	Rhode Island	56.0	592
35	West Virginia	146.5	2,654	35	Minnesota	55.0	2,857
36	Rhode Island	142.8	1,511	36	Idaho	49.2	737
37	Vermont	141.6	880	37	New Hampshire	48.9	643
38	New York	141.0	27,219	38	Alaska	47.0	321
39	Kansas	139.6	3,875	39	Hawaii	45.9	589
40	Alabama	139.4	6,451	40	Nebraska	44.7	793

(Continued)

FRAUD COMPLAINTS BY CONSUMER STATE				IDENTITY THEFT VICTIMS BY STATE			
January 1 - December 31, 2007							
Rank	Consumer State	Complaints Per 100,000 Population	Complaints	Rank	Victim State	Complaints Per 100,000 Population	Complaints
41	South Carolina	137.1	6,041	41	Wisconsin	43.7	2,450
42	New Mexico	136.9	2,697	42	Kentucky	43.3	1,836
43	Iowa	134.3	4,014	43	Wyoming	42.5	222
44	Oklahoma	133.5	4,828	44	Montana	40.8	391
45	Kentucky	129.7	5,502	45	Maine	40.2	530
46	Louisiana	123.9	5,319	46	West Virginia	40.2	729
47	Arkansas	122.8	3,482	47	Vermont	38.1	237
48	North Dakota	113.5	726	48	Iowa	35.6	1,063
49	South Dakota	110.5	880	49	South Dakota	30.8	245
50	Mississippi	90.6	2,644	50	North Dakota	28.5	182

Note: Per 100,000 unit of population estimates are based on the 2007 U.S. Census population estimates (Table NST-EST2007-01 - Annual Estimates of the Population for the United States and States, and for Puerto Rico: April 1, 2000 to July 1, 2007). Numbers for the District of Columbia are: Fraud = 1,375 complaints and 233.7 complaints per 100,000 population; Identity Theft = 784 victims and 133.2 victims per 100,000 population.

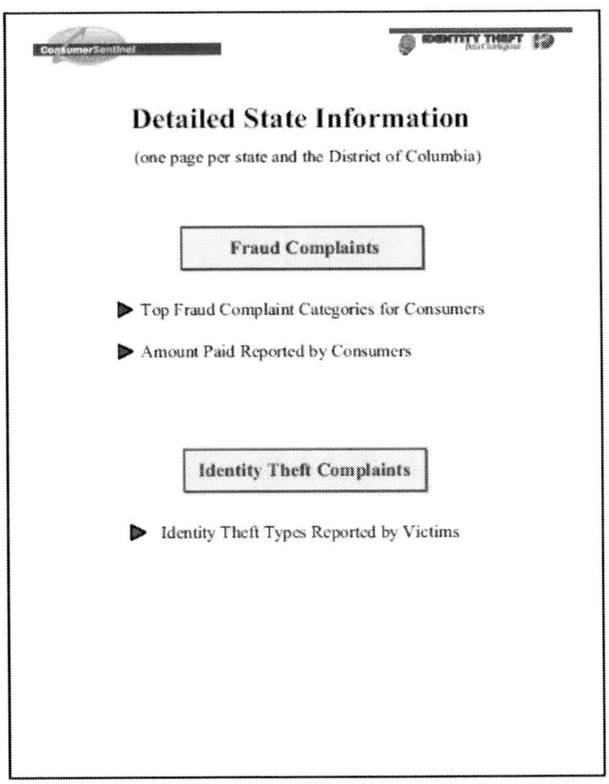

ALABAMA

Consumer Sentinel Complaint Figures
January 1 -December 31, 2007

Total Number of Fraud and Identity Theft Consumer Complaints = 9,672

ConsumerSentinel

Fraud Complaints from Alabama Consumers = 6,451

Top Fraud Complaint Categories for Alabama Consumers

Rank	Top Categories	Complaints	Percentage[1]
1	Shop-at-Home/Catalog Sales	707	11%
2	Prizes/Sweepstakes and Lotteries	458	7%
3	Internet Services	452	7%
4	Foreign Money Offers	366	6%
5	Computer Equipment and Software	303	5%

[1]Percentages are based on the total number of fraud complaints from Alabama consumers (6,451).

Amount Paid Reported by Alabama Consumers

Total No. of Complaints	Total Amount Paid Reported	Total Complaints Reporting Amt Pd	Percentage of Complaints Reporting Amount Paid	Average Amount Paid[2]
6,451	$21,147,725	5,917	92%	$3,574

[2]Average amount paid is based on the total number of fraud complaints where amount paid was reported by Alabama consumers (5,917). Two consumers reported an amount paid of $1 million or more.

IDENTITY THEFT Data Clearinghouse

Identity Theft Complaints from Alabama Victims = 3,221

Identity Theft Types Reported by Alabama Victims

Rank	Identity Theft Type	Complaints	Percentage[1]
1	Government Documents or Benefits Fraud	822	26%
2	Credit Card Fraud	688	21%
3	Phone or Utilities Fraud	484	15%
4	Bank Fraud[2]	371	12%
5	Employment-Related Fraud	247	8%
6	Loan Fraud	180	6%
	Other	745	23%
	Attempted Identity Theft	141	4%

[1]Percentages are based on the 3,221 victims reporting from Alabama. Percentages add to more than 100 because approximately 16% of victims from Alabama reported experiencing more than one type of identity theft.
[2]Includes fraud involving checking and savings accounts and electronic fund transfers.

ALASKA

Consumer Sentinel Complaint Figures
January 1 - December 31, 2007

Total Number of Fraud and Identity Theft Consumer Complaints = 1,753

Fraud Complaints from Alaska Consumers = 1,432

Top Fraud Complaint Categories for Alaska Consumers

Rank	Top Categories	Complaints	Percentage[1]
1	Shop-at-Home/Catalog Sales	161	11%
2	Prizes/Sweepstakes and Lotteries	118	8%
3	Internet Services	111	8%
4	Foreign Money Offers	105	7%
5	Computer Equipment and Software	70	5%

[1]Percentages are based on the total number of fraud complaints from Alaska consumers (1,432).

Amount Paid Reported by Alaska Consumers

Total No. of Complaints	Total Amount Paid Reported	Total Complaints Reporting Amt Pd	Percentage of Complaints Reporting Amount Paid	Average Amount Paid[2]
1,432	$3,266,985	1,269	89%	$2,574

[2]Average amount paid is based on the total number of fraud complaints where amount paid was reported by Alaska consumers (1,269). One consumer reported an amount paid of $2.3 million.

Identity Theft Complaints from Alaska Victims = 321

Identity Theft Types Reported by Alaska Victims

Rank	Identity Theft Type	Complaints	Percentage[1]
1	Credit Card Fraud	72	22%
2	Phone or Utilities Fraud	50	16%
3	Bank Fraud[2]	46	14%
4	Employment-Related Fraud	29	9%
5	Government Documents or Benefits Fraud	21	7%
6	Loan Fraud	20	6%
	Other	94	29%
	Attempted Identity Theft	14	4%

[1]Percentages are based on the 321 victims reporting from Alaska. Percentages add to more than 100 because approximately 12% of victims from Alaska reported experiencing more than one type of identity theft.
[2]Includes fraud involving checking and savings accounts and electronic fund transfers.

ARIZONA

Consumer Sentinel Complaint Figures
January 1 - December 31, 2007

Total Number of Fraud and Identity Theft Consumer Complaints = 22,591

ConsumerSentinel

Fraud Complaints from Arizona Consumers = 13,903

Top Fraud Complaint Categories for Arizona Consumers

Rank	Top Categories	Complaints	Percentage[1]
1	Shop-at-Home/Catalog Sales	1,325	10%
2	Internet Services	961	7%
3	Foreign Money Offers	737	5%
4	Prizes/Sweepstakes and Lotteries	728	5%
5	Health Care	610	4%

[1]Percentages are based on the total number of fraud complaints from Arizona consumers (13,903).

Amount Paid Reported by Arizona Consumers

Total No. of Complaints	Total Amount Paid Reported	Total Complaints Reporting Amt Pd	Percentage of Complaints Reporting Amount Paid	Average Amount Paid[2]
13,903	$31,203,092	12,614	91%	$2,474

[2]Average amount paid is based on the total number of fraud complaints where amount paid was reported by Arizona consumers (12,614). Four consumers reported an amount paid of $1 million or more.

IDENTITY THEFT

Identity Theft Complaints from Arizona Victims = 8,688

Identity Theft Types Reported by Arizona Victims

Rank	Identity Theft Type	Complaints	Percentage[1]
1	Employment-Related Fraud	3,122	36%
2	Credit Card Fraud	1,388	16%
3	Bank Fraud[2]	1,008	12%
4	Phone or Utilities Fraud	996	11%
5	Government Documents or Benefits Fraud	573	7%
6	Loan Fraud	414	5%
	Other	2,032	23%
	Attempted Identity Theft	353	4%

[1]Percentages are based on the 8,688 victims reporting from Arizona. Percentages add to more than 100 because approximately 15% of victims from Arizona reported experiencing more than one type of identity theft.

[2]Includes fraud involving checking and savings accounts and electronic fund transfers.

ARKANSAS

Consumer Sentinel Complaint Figures
January 1 - December 31, 2007

Total Number of Fraud and Identity Theft Consumer Complaints = 5,083

ConsumerSentinel

Fraud Complaints from Arkansas Consumers = 3,482

Top Fraud Complaint Categories for Arkansas Consumers

Rank	Top Categories	Complaints	Percentage[1]
1	Shop-at-Home/Catalog Sales	398	11%
2	Internet Services	236	7%
3	Internet Auctions	184	5%
4	Foreign Money Offers	178	5%
5	Prizes/Sweepstakes and Lotteries	166	5%

[1]Percentages are based on the total number of fraud complaints from Arkansas consumers (3,482).

Amount Paid Reported by Arkansas Consumers

Total No. of Complaints	Total Amount Paid Reported	Total Complaints Reporting Amt Pd	Percentage of Complaints Reporting Amount Paid	Average Amount Paid[2]
3,482	$19,118,209	3,176	91%	$6,020

[2]Average amount paid is based on the total number of fraud complaints where amount paid was reported by Arkansas consumers (3,176). Five consumers reported an amount paid of $1 million or more.

IDENTITY THEFT Data Clearinghouse

Identity Theft Complaints from Arkansas Victims = 1,601

Identity Theft Types Reported by Arkansas Victims

Rank	Identity Theft Type	Complaints	Percentage[1]
1	Credit Card Fraud	380	24%
2	Phone or Utilities Fraud	289	18%
3	Bank Fraud[2]	262	16%
4	Government Documents or Benefits Fraud	196	12%
5	Employment-Related Fraud	139	9%
6	Loan Fraud	79	5%
	Other	399	25%
	Attempted Identity Theft	72	4%

[1]Percentages are based on the 1,601 victims reporting from Arkansas. Percentages add to more than 100 because approximately 17% of victims from Arkansas reported experiencing more than one type of identity theft.
[2]Includes fraud involving checking and savings accounts and electronic fund transfers.

CALIFORNIA

Consumer Sentinel Complaint Figures
January 1 - December 31, 2007

Total Number of Fraud and Identity Theft Consumer Complaints = 105,301

ConsumerSentinel

Fraud Complaints from California Consumers = 61,409

Top Fraud Complaint Categories for California Consumers

Rank	Top Categories	Complaints	Percentage[1]
1	Shop-at-Home/Catalog Sales	6,591	11%
2	Internet Services	5,629	9%
3	Foreign Money Offers	4,485	7%
4	Prizes/Sweepstakes and Lotteries	3,678	6%
5	Computer Equipment and Software	2,993	5%

[1]Percentages are based on the total number of fraud complaints from California consumers (61,409).

Amount Paid Reported by California Consumers

Total No. of Complaints	Total Amount Paid Reported	Total Complaints Reporting Amt Pd	Percentage of Complaints Reporting Amount Paid	Average Amount Paid[2]
61,409	$171,420,647	54,315	88%	$3,156

[2]Average amount paid is based on the total number of fraud complaints where amount paid was reported by California consumers (54,315). Thirty-five consumers reported an amount paid of $1 million or more.

IDENTITY THEFT

Identity Theft Complaints from California Victims = 43,892

Identity Theft Types Reported by California Victims

Rank	Identity Theft Type	Complaints	Percentage[1]
1	Credit Card Fraud	9,883	23%
2	Employment-Related Fraud	7,832	18%
3	Phone or Utilities Fraud	7,729	18%
4	Bank Fraud[2]	6,238	14%
5	Government Documents or Benefits Fraud	3,537	8%
6	Loan Fraud	2,045	5%
	Other	11,097	25%
	Attempted Identity Theft	2,107	5%

[1]Percentages are based on the 43,892 victims reporting from California. Percentages add to more than 100 because approximately 17% of victims from California reported experiencing more than one type of identity theft.
[2]Includes fraud involving checking and savings accounts and electronic fund transfers.

COLORADO

Consumer Sentinel Complaint Figures
January 1 - December 31, 2007

Total Number of Fraud and Identity Theft Consumer Complaints = 15,692

ConsumerSentinel

Fraud Complaints from Colorado Consumers = 11,364

Top Fraud Complaint Categories for Colorado Consumers

Rank	Top Categories	Complaints	Percentage[1]
1	Shop-at-Home/Catalog Sales	1,162	10%
2	Internet Services	939	8%
3	Foreign Money Offers	743	7%
4	Computer Equipment and Software	574	5%
5	Internet Auctions	520	5%

[1]Percentages are based on the total number of fraud complaints from Colorado consumers (11,364).

Amount Paid Reported by Colorado Consumers

Total No. of Complaints	Total Amount Paid Reported	Total Complaints Reporting Amt Pd	Percentage of Complaints Reporting Amount Paid	Average Amount Paid[2]
11,364	$41,318,939	10,225	90%	$4,041

[2]Average amount paid is based on the total number of fraud complaints where amount paid was reported by Colorado consumers (10,225). Fourteen consumers reported an amount paid of $1 million or more.

IDENTITY THEFT Data Clearinghouse

Identity Theft Complaints from Colorado Victims = 4,328

Identity Theft Types Reported by Colorado Victims

Rank	Identity Theft Type	Complaints	Percentage[1]
1	Employment-Related Fraud	911	21%
2	Credit Card Fraud	872	20%
3	Phone or Utilities Fraud	636	15%
4	Bank Fraud[2]	599	14%
5	Government Documents or Benefits Fraud	312	7%
6	Loan Fraud	195	5%
	Other	1,256	29%
	Attempted Identity Theft	216	5%

[1]Percentages are based on the 4,328 victims reporting from Colorado. Percentages add to more than 100 because approximately 16% of victims from Colorado reported experiencing more than one type of identity theft.
[2]Includes fraud involving checking and savings accounts and electronic fund transfers.

CONNECTICUT

Consumer Sentinel Complaint Figures
January 1 - December 31, 2007

Total Number of Fraud and Identity Theft Consumer Complaints = 7,673

ConsumerSentinel

Fraud Complaints from Connecticut Consumers = 5,264

Top Fraud Complaint Categories for Connecticut Consumers

Rank	Top Categories	Complaints	Percentage[1]
1	Shop-at-Home/Catalog Sales	746	14%
2	Prizes/Sweepstakes and Lotteries	499	9%
3	Foreign Money Offers	409	8%
4	Internet Services	360	7%
5	Internet Auctions	342	6%

[1]Percentages are based on the total number of fraud complaints from Connecticut consumers (5,264).

Amount Paid Reported by Connecticut Consumers

Total No. of Complaints	Total Amount Paid Reported	Total Complaints Reporting Amt Pd	Percentage of Complaints Reporting Amount Paid	Average Amount Paid[2]
5,264	$5,817,263	4,730	90%	$1,230

[2]Average amount paid is based on the total number of fraud complaints where amount paid was reported by Connecticut consumers (4,730).

IDENTITY THEFT Data Clearinghouse

Identity Theft Complaints from Connecticut Victims = 2,409

Identity Theft Types Reported by Connecticut Victims

Rank	Identity Theft Type	Complaints	Percentage[1]
1	Credit Card Fraud	621	26%
2	Phone or Utilities Fraud	441	18%
3	Bank Fraud[2]	361	15%
4	Employment-Related Fraud	238	10%
5	Government Documents or Benefits Fraud	195	8%
6	Loan Fraud	104	4%
	Other	661	27%
	Attempted Identity Theft	151	6%

[1]Percentages are based on the 2,409 victims reporting from Connecticut. Percentages add to more than 100 because approximately 17% of victims from Connecticut reported experiencing more than one type of identity theft.
[2]Includes fraud involving checking and savings accounts and electronic fund transfers.

DELAWARE

Consumer Sentinel Complaint Figures
January 1 - December 31, 2007

Total Number of Fraud and Identity Theft Consumer Complaints = 1,944

ConsumerSentinel

Fraud Complaints from Delaware Consumers = 1,341

Top Fraud Complaint Categories for Delaware Consumers

Rank	Top Categories	Complaints	Percentage[1]
1	Shop-at-Home/Catalog Sales	146	11%
2	Internet Services	122	9%
3	Foreign Money Offers	102	8%
4	Prizes/Sweepstakes and Lotteries	92	7%
5	Internet Auctions	88	7%

[1]Percentages are based on the total number of fraud complaints from Delaware consumers (1,341).

Amount Paid Reported by Delaware Consumers

Total No. of Complaints	Total Amount Paid Reported	Total Complaints Reporting Amt Pd	Percentage of Complaints Reporting Amount Paid	Average Amount Paid[2]
1,341	$1,223,658	1,187	89%	$1,031

[2]Average amount paid is based on the total number of fraud complaints where amount paid was reported by Delaware consumers (1,187).

IDENTITY THEFT Data Clearinghouse

Identity Theft Complaints from Delaware Victims = 603

Identity Theft Types Reported by Delaware Victims

Rank	Identity Theft Type	Complaints	Percentage[1]
1	Phone or Utilities Fraud	139	23%
2	Credit Card Fraud	138	23%
3	Employment-Related Fraud	72	12%
4	Government Documents or Benefits Fraud	58	10%
5	Bank Fraud[2]	57	9%
6	Loan Fraud	27	4%
	Other	154	26%
	Attempted Identity Theft	31	5%

[1]Percentages are based on the 603 victims reporting from Delaware. Percentages add to more than 100 because approximately 14% of victims from Delaware reported experiencing more than one type of identity theft.

[2]Includes fraud involving checking and savings accounts and electronic fund transfers.

DISTRICT OF COLUMBIA

Consumer Sentinel Complaint Figures
January 1 - December 31, 2007

Total Number of Fraud and Identity Theft Consumer Complaints = 2,159

ConsumerSentinel

Fraud Complaints from District of Columbia Consumers = 1,375

Top Fraud Complaint Categories for District of Columbia Consumers

Rank	Top Categories	Complaints	Percentage[1]
1	Shop-at-Home/Catalog Sales	154	11%
2	Internet Services	137	10%
3	Prizes/Sweepstakes and Lotteries	93	7%
4	Foreign Money Offers	84	6%
5	Computer Equipment and Software	71	5%

[1]Percentages are based on the total number of fraud complaints from District of Columbia consumers (1,375).

Amount Paid Reported by District of Columbia Consumers

Total No. of Complaints	Total Amount Paid Reported	Total Complaints Reporting Amt Pd	Percentage of Complaints Reporting Amount Paid	Average Amount Paid[2]
1,375	$3,681,326	1,187	86%	$3,101

[2]Average amount paid is based on the total number of fraud complaints where amount paid was reported by District of Columbia consumers (1,187). Two consumers reported an amount paid of $1 million or more.

IDENTITY THEFT

Identity Theft Complaints from District of Columbia Victims = 784

Identity Theft Types Reported by District of Columbia Victims

Rank	Identity Theft Type	Complaints	Percentage[1]
1	Credit Card Fraud	193	25%
2	Phone or Utilities Fraud	136	17%
3	Bank Fraud[2]	130	17%
4	Government Documents or Benefits Fraud	92	12%
5	Loan Fraud	52	7%
6	Employment-Related Fraud	43	5%
	Other	198	25%
	Attempted Identity Theft	41	5%

[1]Percentages are based on the 784 victims reporting from the District of Columbia. Percentages add to more than 100 because approximately 16% of victims from the District of Columbia reported experiencing more than one type of identity theft.
[2]Includes fraud involving checking and savings accounts and electronic fund transfers.

FLORIDA

Consumer Sentinel Complaint Figures
January 1 - December 31, 2007

Total Number of Fraud and Identity Theft Consumer Complaints = 52,297

ConsumerSentinel

Fraud Complaints from Florida Consumers = 33,027

Top Fraud Complaint Categories for Florida Consumers

Rank	Top Categories	Complaints	Percentage[1]
1	Shop-at-Home/Catalog Sales	3,572	11%
2	Internet Services	2,691	8%
3	Foreign Money Offers	2,210	7%
4	Prizes/Sweepstakes and Lotteries	1,894	6%
5	Internet Auctions	1,763	5%

[1]Percentages are based on the total number of fraud complaints from Florida consumers (33,027).

Amount Paid Reported by Florida Consumers

Total No. of Complaints	Total Amount Paid Reported	Total Complaints Reporting Amt Pd	Percentage of Complaints Reporting Amount Paid	Average Amount Paid[2]
33,027	$60,469,285	29,386	89%	$2,058

[2]Average amount paid is based on the total number of fraud complaints where amount paid was reported by Florida consumers (29,386). Eight consumers reported an amount paid of $1 million or more.

IDENTITY THEFT Data Clearinghouse

Identity Theft Complaints from Florida Victims = 19,270

Identity Theft Types Reported by Florida Victims

Rank	Identity Theft Type	Complaints	Percentage[1]
1	Credit Card Fraud	4,406	23%
2	Phone or Utilities Fraud	3,090	16%
3	Bank Fraud[2]	2,878	15%
4	Government Documents or Benefits Fraud	2,753	14%
5	Employment-Related Fraud	1,744	9%
6	Loan Fraud	967	5%
	Other	5,186	27%
	Attempted Identity Theft	1,020	5%

[1]Percentages are based on the 19,270 victims reporting from Florida. Percentages add to more than 100 because approximately 17% of victims from Florida reported experiencing more than one type of identity theft.
[2]Includes fraud involving checking and savings accounts and electronic fund transfers.

GEORGIA

Consumer Sentinel Complaint Figures
January 1 - December 31, 2007

Total Number of Fraud and Identity Theft Consumer Complaints = 24,680

ConsumerSentinel

Fraud Complaints from Georgia Consumers = 15,936

Top Fraud Complaint Categories for Georgia Consumers

Rank	Top Categories	Complaints	Percentage[1]
1	Shop-at-Home/Catalog Sales	1,617	10%
2	Internet Services	1,182	7%
3	Foreign Money Offers	975	6%
4	Prizes/Sweepstakes and Lotteries	891	6%
5	Computer Equipment and Software	779	5%

[1]Percentages are based on the total number of fraud complaints from Georgia consumers (15,936).

Amount Paid Reported by Georgia Consumers

Total No. of Complaints	Total Amount Paid Reported	Total Complaints Reporting Amt Pd	Percentage of Complaints Reporting Amount Paid	Average Amount Paid[2]
15,936	$21,544,911	14,402	90%	$1,496

[2]Average amount paid is based on the total number of fraud complaints where amount paid was reported by Georgia consumers (14,402). Two consumers reported an amount paid of $1 million or more.

IDENTITY THEFT Data Clearinghouse

Identity Theft Complaints from Georgia Victims = 8,744

Identity Theft Types Reported by Georgia Victims

Rank	Identity Theft Type	Complaints	Percentage[1]
1	Credit Card Fraud	1,918	22%
2	Phone or Utilities Fraud	1,453	17%
3	Government Documents or Benefits Fraud	1,405	16%
4	Bank Fraud[2]	1,311	15%
5	Employment-Related Fraud	793	9%
6	Loan Fraud	445	5%
	Other	2,253	26%
	Attempted Identity Theft	448	5%

[1]Percentages are based on the 8,744 victims reporting from Georgia. Percentages add to more than 100 because approximately 16% of victims from Georgia reported experiencing more than one type of identity theft.

[2]Includes fraud involving checking and savings accounts and electronic fund transfers.

HAWAII

Consumer Sentinel Complaint Figures
January 1 - December 31, 2007

Total Number of Fraud and Identity Theft Consumer Complaints = 3,109

ConsumerSentinel

Fraud Complaints from Hawaii Consumers = 2,520

Top Fraud Complaint Categories for Hawaii Consumers

Rank	Top Categories	Complaints	Percentage[1]
1	Shop-at-Home/Catalog Sales	341	14%
2	Prizes/Sweepstakes and Lotteries	206	8%
3	Internet Services	198	8%
4	Internet Auctions	168	7%
5	Foreign Money Offers	166	7%

[1]Percentages are based on the total number of fraud complaints from Hawaii consumers (2,520).

Amount Paid Reported by Hawaii Consumers

Total No. of Complaints	Total Amount Paid Reported	Total Complaints Reporting Amt Pd	Percentage of Complaints Reporting Amount Paid	Average Amount Paid[2]
2,520	$3,264,418	2,252	89%	$1,450

[2]Average amount paid is based on the total number of fraud complaints where amount paid was reported by Hawaii consumers (2,252).

IDENTITY THEFT

Identity Theft Complaints from Hawaii Victims = 589

Identity Theft Types Reported by Hawaii Victims

Rank	Identity Theft Type	Complaints	Percentage[1]
1	Credit Card Fraud	219	37%
2	Bank Fraud[2]	99	17%
3	Phone or Utilities Fraud	76	13%
4	Employment-Related Fraud	37	6%
5	Government Documents or Benefits Fraud	25	4%
6	Loan Fraud	25	4%
	Other	162	28%
	Attempted Identity Theft	21	4%

[1]Percentages are based on the 589 victims reporting from Hawaii. Percentages add to more than 100 because approximately 15% of victims from Hawaii reported experiencing more than one type of identity theft.
[2]Includes fraud involving checking and savings accounts and electronic fund transfers.

IDAHO

Consumer Sentinel Complaint Figures
January 1 - December 31, 2007

Total Number of Fraud and Identity Theft Consumer Complaints = 3,300

ConsumerSentinel

Fraud Complaints from Idaho Consumers = 2,563

Top Fraud Complaint Categories for Idaho Consumers

Rank	Top Categories	Complaints	Percentage[1]
1	Shop-at-Home/Catalog Sales	276	11%
2	Internet Services	229	9%
3	Foreign Money Offers	148	6%
4	Prizes/Sweepstakes and Lotteries	134	5%
5	Internet Auctions	129	5%

[1]Percentages are based on the total number of fraud complaints from Idaho consumers (2,563).

Amount Paid Reported by Idaho Consumers

Total No. of Complaints	Total Amount Paid Reported	Total Complaints Reporting Amt Pd	Percentage of Complaints Reporting Amount Paid	Average Amount Paid[2]
2,563	$2,383,129	2,318	90%	$1,028

[2]Average amount paid is based on the total number of fraud complaints where amount paid was reported by Idaho consumers (2,318).

IDENTITY THEFT Data Clearinghouse

Identity Theft Complaints from Idaho Victims = 737

Identity Theft Types Reported by Idaho Victims

Rank	Identity Theft Type	Complaints	Percentage[1]
1	Credit Card Fraud	160	22%
2	Phone or Utilities Fraud	136	18%
3	Employment-Related Fraud	84	11%
4	Bank Fraud[2]	80	11%
5	Government Documents or Benefits Fraud	54	7%
6	Loan Fraud	32	4%
	Other	227	31%
	Attempted Identity Theft	39	5%

[1]Percentages are based on the 737 victims reporting from Idaho. Percentages add to more than 100 because approximately 13% of victims from Idaho reported experiencing more than one type of identity theft.

[2]Includes fraud involving checking and savings accounts and electronic fund transfers.

ILLINOIS

Consumer Sentinel Complaint Figures
January 1 - December 31, 2007

Total Number of Fraud and Identity Theft Consumer Complaints = 31,906

ConsumerSentinel

Fraud Complaints from Illinois Consumers = 21,602

Top Fraud Complaint Categories for Illinois Consumers

Rank	Top Categories	Complaints	Percentage[1]
1	Shop-at-Home/Catalog Sales	2,227	10%
2	Internet Services	1,588	7%
3	Computer Equipment and Software	1,173	5%
4	Foreign Money Offers	1,105	5%
5	Prizes/Sweepstakes and Lotteries	1,058	5%

[1]Percentages are based on the total number of fraud complaints from Illinois consumers (21,602).

Amount Paid Reported by Illinois Consumers

Total No. of Complaints	Total Amount Paid Reported	Total Complaints Reporting Amt Pd	Percentage of Complaints Reporting Amount Paid	Average Amount Paid[2]
21,602	$38,585,928	19,807	92%	$1,948

[2]Average amount paid is based on the total number of fraud complaints where amount paid was reported by Illinois consumers (19,807). Six consumers reported an amount paid of $1 million or more.

IDENTITY THEFT Data Clearinghouse

Identity Theft Complaints from Illinois Victims = 10,304

Identity Theft Types Reported by Illinois Victims

Rank	Identity Theft Type	Complaints	Percentage[1]
1	Credit Card Fraud	2,345	23%
2	Phone or Utilities Fraud	1,945	19%
3	Employment-Related Fraud	1,460	14%
4	Government Documents or Benefits Fraud	1,287	12%
5	Bank Fraud[2]	1,271	12%
6	Loan Fraud	551	5%
	Other	2,481	24%
	Attempted Identity Theft	526	5%

[1]Percentages are based on the 10,304 victims reporting from Illinois. Percentages add to more than 100 because approximately 17% of victims from Illinois reported experiencing more than one type of identity theft.
[2]Includes fraud involving checking and savings accounts and electronic fund transfers.

INDIANA

Consumer Sentinel Complaint Figures
January 1 - December 31, 2007

Total Number of Fraud and Identity Theft Consumer Complaints = 14,431

ConsumerSentinel

Fraud Complaints from Indiana Consumers = 10,405

Top Fraud Complaint Categories for Indiana Consumers

Rank	Top Categories	Complaints	Percentage[1]
1	Shop-at-Home/Catalog Sales	1,068	10%
2	Prizes/Sweepstakes and Lotteries	1,012	10%
3	Internet Services	716	7%
4	Foreign Money Offers	676	6%
5	Computer Equipment and Software	419	4%

[1]Percentages are based on the total number of fraud complaints from Indiana consumers (10,405).

Amount Paid Reported by Indiana Consumers

Total No. of Complaints	Total Amount Paid Reported	Total Complaints Reporting Amt Pd	Percentage of Complaints Reporting Amount Paid	Average Amount Paid[2]
10,405	$18,607,786	9,463	91%	$1,966

[2]Average amount paid is based on the total number of fraud complaints where amount paid was reported by Indiana consumers (9,463). Two consumers reported an amount paid of $1 million or more.

IDENTITY THEFT

Identity Theft Complaints from Indiana Victims = 4,026

Identity Theft Types Reported by Indiana Victims

Rank	Identity Theft Type	Complaints	Percentage[1]
1	Phone or Utilities Fraud	1,007	25%
2	Credit Card Fraud	806	20%
3	Bank Fraud[2]	549	14%
4	Government Documents or Benefits Fraud	423	11%
5	Employment-Related Fraud	418	10%
6	Loan Fraud	195	5%
	Other	965	24%
	Attempted Identity Theft	205	5%

[1]Percentages are based on the 4,026 victims reporting from Indiana. Percentages add to more than 100 because approximately 16% of victims from Indiana reported experiencing more than one type of identity theft.

[2]Includes fraud involving checking and savings accounts and electronic fund transfers.

IOWA

Consumer Sentinel Complaint Figures
January 1 - December 31, 2007

Total Number of Fraud and Identity Theft Consumer Complaints = 5,077

ConsumerSentinel

Fraud Complaints from Iowa Consumers = 4,014

Top Fraud Complaint Categories for Iowa Consumers

Rank	Top Categories	Complaints	Percentage[1]
1	Shop-at-Home/Catalog Sales	503	13%
2	Internet Services	299	7%
3	Internet Auctions	223	6%
4	Foreign Money Offers	221	6%
5	Computer Equipment and Software	212	5%

[1]Percentages are based on the total number of fraud complaints from Iowa consumers (4,014).

Amount Paid Reported by Iowa Consumers

Total No. of Complaints	Total Amount Paid Reported	Total Complaints Reporting Amt Pd	Percentage of Complaints Reporting Amount Paid	Average Amount Paid[2]
4,014	$2,604,987	3,654	91%	$713

[2]Average amount paid is based on the total number of fraud complaints where amount paid was reported by Iowa consumers (3,654).

IDENTITY THEFT Data Clearinghouse

Identity Theft Complaints from Iowa Victims = 1,063

Identity Theft Types Reported by Iowa Victims

Rank	Identity Theft Type	Complaints	Percentage[1]
1	Credit Card Fraud	296	28%
2	Phone or Utilities Fraud	180	17%
3	Bank Fraud[2]	137	13%
4	Employment-Related Fraud	110	10%
5	Government Documents or Benefits Fraud	77	7%
6	Loan Fraud	46	4%
	Other	278	26%
	Attempted Identity Theft	54	5%

[1]Percentages are based on the 1,063 victims reporting from Iowa. Percentages add to more than 100 because approximately 14% of victims from Iowa reported experiencing more than one type of identity theft.
[2]Includes fraud involving checking and savings accounts and electronic fund transfers.

KANSAS

Consumer Sentinel Complaint Figures
January 1 - December 31, 2007

Total Number of Fraud and Identity Theft Consumer Complaints = 5,569

ConsumerSentinel

Fraud Complaints from Kansas Consumers = 3,875

Top Fraud Complaint Categories for Kansas Consumers

Rank	Top Categories	Complaints	Percentage[1]
1	Shop-at-Home/Catalog Sales	462	12%
2	Foreign Money Offers	259	7%
3	Internet Services	252	7%
4	Internet Auctions	203	5%
5	Computer Equipment and Software	203	5%

[1]Percentages are based on the total number of fraud complaints from Kansas consumers (3,875).

Amount Paid Reported by Kansas Consumers

Total No. of Complaints	Total Amount Paid Reported	Total Complaints Reporting Amt Pd	Percentage of Complaints Reporting Amount Paid	Average Amount Paid[2]
3,875	$16,518,673	3,500	90%	$4,720

[2]Average amount paid is based on the total number of fraud complaints where amount paid was reported by Kansas consumers (3,500). Three consumers reported an amount paid of $1 million or more.

IDENTITY THEFT Data Clearinghouse

Identity Theft Complaints from Kansas Victims = 1,694

Identity Theft Types Reported by Kansas Victims

Rank	Identity Theft Type	Complaints	Percentage[1]
1	Credit Card Fraud	424	25%
2	Bank Fraud[2]	288	17%
3	Phone or Utilities Fraud	268	16%
4	Employment-Related Fraud	220	13%
5	Government Documents or Benefits Fraud	133	8%
6	Loan Fraud	82	5%
	Other	432	26%
	Attempted Identity Theft	88	5%

[1]Percentages are based on the 1,694 victims reporting from Kansas. Percentages add to more than 100 because approximately 16% of victims from Kansas reported experiencing more than one type of identity theft.
[2]Includes fraud involving checking and savings accounts and electronic fund transfers.

KENTUCKY

Consumer Sentinel Complaint Figures
January 1 - December 31, 2007

Total Number of Fraud and Identity Theft Consumer Complaints = 7,338

Fraud Complaints from Kentucky Consumers = 5,502

Top Fraud Complaint Categories for Kentucky Consumers

Rank	Top Categories	Complaints	Percentage[1]
1	Shop-at-Home/Catalog Sales	696	13%
2	Internet Services	403	7%
3	Prizes/Sweepstakes and Lotteries	356	6%
4	Foreign Money Offers	319	6%
5	Computer Equipment and Software	309	6%

[1]Percentages are based on the total number of fraud complaints from Kentucky consumers (5,502).

Amount Paid Reported by Kentucky Consumers

Total No. of Complaints	Total Amount Paid Reported	Total Complaints Reporting Amt Pd	Percentage of Complaints Reporting Amount Paid	Average Amount Paid[2]
5,502	$6,777,987	4,987	91%	$1,359

[2]Average amount paid is based on the total number of fraud complaints where amount paid was reported by Kentucky consumers (4,987). One consumer reported an amount paid of $1.6 million.

Identity Theft Complaints from Kentucky Victims = 1,836

Identity Theft Types Reported by Kentucky Victims

Rank	Identity Theft Type	Complaints	Percentage[1]
1	Credit Card Fraud	484	26%
2	Phone or Utilities Fraud	396	22%
3	Bank Fraud[2]	251	14%
4	Government Documents or Benefits Fraud	178	10%
5	Employment-Related Fraud	156	8%
6	Loan Fraud	77	4%
	Other	446	24%
	Attempted Identity Theft	101	6%

[1]Percentages are based on the 1,836 victims reporting from Kentucky. Percentages add to more than 100 because approximately 16% of victims from Kentucky reported experiencing more than one type of identity theft.
[2]Includes fraud involving checking and savings accounts and electronic fund transfers.

Louisiana

Consumer Sentinel Complaint Figures
January 1 - December 31, 2007

Total Number of Fraud and Identity Theft Consumer Complaints = 7,993

ConsumerSentinel

Fraud Complaints from Louisiana Consumers = 5,319

Top Fraud Complaint Categories for Louisiana Consumers

Rank	Top Categories	Complaints	Percentage[1]
1	Shop-at-Home/Catalog Sales	658	12%
2	Foreign Money Offers	350	7%
3	Prizes/Sweepstakes and Lotteries	347	7%
4	Internet Services	308	6%
5	Internet Auctions	264	5%

[1]Percentages are based on the total number of fraud complaints from Louisiana consumers (5,319).

Amount Paid Reported by Louisiana Consumers

Total No. of Complaints	Total Amount Paid Reported	Total Complaints Reporting Amt Pd	Percentage of Complaints Reporting Amount Paid	Average Amount Paid[2]
5,319	$10,679,438	4,883	92%	$2,187

[2]Average amount paid is based on the total number of fraud complaints where amount paid was reported by Louisiana consumers (4,883). Two consumers reported an amount paid of $1 million or more.

IDENTITY THEFT Data Clearinghouse

Identity Theft Complaints from Louisiana Victims = 2,674

Identity Theft Types Reported by Louisiana Victims

Rank	Identity Theft Type	Complaints	Percentage[1]
1	Government Documents or Benefits Fraud	597	22%
2	Credit Card Fraud	579	22%
3	Phone or Utilities Fraud	488	18%
4	Bank Fraud[2]	346	13%
5	Employment-Related Fraud	203	8%
6	Loan Fraud	136	5%
	Other	561	21%
	Attempted Identity Theft	129	5%

[1]Percentages are based on the 2,674 victims reporting from Louisiana. Percentages add to more than 100 because approximately 16% of victims from Louisiana reported experiencing more than one type of identity theft.

[2]Includes fraud involving checking and savings accounts and electronic fund transfers.

MAINE

Consumer Sentinel Complaint Figures
January 1 - December 31, 2007

Total Number of Fraud and Identity Theft Consumer Complaints = 2,641

ConsumerSentinel

Fraud Complaints from Maine Consumers = 2,111

Top Fraud Complaint Categories for Maine Consumers

Rank	Top Categories	Complaints	Percentage[1]
1	Shop-at-Home/Catalog Sales	435	21%
2	Internet Services	145	7%
3	Foreign Money Offers	142	7%
4	Prizes/Sweepstakes and Lotteries	136	6%
5	Internet Auctions	97	5%

[1]Percentages are based on the total number of fraud complaints from Maine consumers (2,111).

Amount Paid Reported by Maine Consumers

Total No. of Complaints	Total Amount Paid Reported	Total Complaints Reporting Amt Pd	Percentage of Complaints Reporting Amount Paid	Average Amount Paid[2]
2,111	$9,438,733	1,873	89%	$5,039

[2]Average amount paid is based on the total number of fraud complaints where amount paid was reported by Maine consumers (1,873). One consumer reported an amount paid of $8 million.

IDENTITY THEFT Data Clearinghouse

Identity Theft Complaints from Maine Victims = 530

Identity Theft Types Reported by Maine Victims

Rank	Identity Theft Type	Complaints	Percentage[1]
1	Credit Card Fraud	162	31%
2	Phone or Utilities Fraud	86	16%
3	Bank Fraud[2]	75	14%
4	Employment-Related Fraud	29	5%
5	Government Documents or Benefits Fraud	24	5%
6	Loan Fraud	22	4%
	Other	152	29%
	Attempted Identity Theft	36	7%

[1]Percentages are based on the 530 victims reporting from Maine. Percentages add to more than 100 because approximately 14% of victims from Maine reported experiencing more than one type of identity theft.
[2]Includes fraud involving checking and savings accounts and electronic fund transfers.

MARYLAND

Consumer Sentinel Complaint Figures
January 1 - December 31, 2007

Total Number of Fraud and Identity Theft Consumer Complaints = 16,566

ConsumerSentinel

Fraud Complaints from Maryland Consumers = 11,745

Top Fraud Complaint Categories for Maryland Consumers

Rank	Top Categories	Complaints	Percentage[1]
1	Shop-at-Home/Catalog Sales	1,314	11%
2	Foreign Money Offers	980	8%
3	Internet Services	905	8%
4	Prizes/Sweepstakes and Lotteries	640	5%
5	Computer Equipment and Software	622	5%

[1]Percentages are based on the total number of fraud complaints from Maryland consumers (11,745).

Amount Paid Reported by Maryland Consumers

Total No. of Complaints	Total Amount Paid Reported	Total Complaints Reporting Amt Pd	Percentage of Complaints Reporting Amount Paid	Average Amount Paid[2]
11,745	$17,223,500	10,549	90%	$1,633

[2]Average amount paid is based on the total number of fraud complaints where amount paid was reported by Maryland consumers (10,549). Two consumers reported an amount paid of $1 million or more.

IDENTITY THEFT Data Clearinghouse

Identity Theft Complaints from Maryland Victims = 4,821

Identity Theft Types Reported by Maryland Victims

Rank	Identity Theft Type	Complaints	Percentage[1]
1	Credit Card Fraud	1,362	28%
2	Phone or Utilities Fraud	908	19%
3	Bank Fraud[2]	741	15%
4	Government Documents or Benefits Fraud	389	8%
5	Employment-Related Fraud	295	6%
6	Loan Fraud	239	5%
	Other	1,224	25%
	Attempted Identity Theft	265	5%

[1]Percentages are based on the 4,821 victims reporting from Maryland. Percentages add to more than 100 because approximately 14% of victims from Maryland reported experiencing more than one type of identity theft.
[2]Includes fraud involving checking and savings accounts and electronic fund transfers.

MASSACHUSETTS

Consumer Sentinel Complaint Figures
January 1 - December 31, 2007

Total Number of Fraud and Identity Theft Consumer Complaints = 14,058

ConsumerSentinel

Fraud Complaints from Massachusetts Consumers = 9,766

Top Fraud Complaint Categories for Massachusetts Consumers

Rank	Top Categories	Complaints	Percentage[1]
1	Shop-at-Home/Catalog Sales	1,196	12%
2	Internet Services	802	8%
3	Foreign Money Offers	678	7%
4	Computer Equipment and Software	673	7%
5	Prizes/Sweepstakes and Lotteries	491	5%

[1]Percentages are based on the total number of fraud complaints from Massachusetts consumers (9,766).

Amount Paid Reported by Massachusetts Consumers

Total No. of Complaints	Total Amount Paid Reported	Total Complaints Reporting Amt Pd	Percentage of Complaints Reporting Amount Paid	Average Amount Paid[2]
9,766	$13,342,766	8,738	89%	$1,527

[2]Average amount paid is based on the total number of fraud complaints where amount paid was reported by Massachusetts consumers (8,738). Three consumers reported an amount paid of $1 million or more.

IDENTITY THEFT Data Clearinghouse

Identity Theft Complaints from Massachusetts Victims = 4,292

Identity Theft Types Reported by Massachusetts Victims

Rank	Identity Theft Type	Complaints	Percentage[1]
1	Credit Card Fraud	1,266	29%
2	Phone or Utilities Fraud	791	18%
3	Bank Fraud[2]	553	13%
4	Employment-Related Fraud	434	10%
5	Government Documents or Benefits Fraud	335	8%
6	Loan Fraud	182	4%
	Other	1,081	25%
	Attempted Identity Theft	275	6%

[1]Percentages are based on the 4,292 victims reporting from Massachusetts. Percentages add to more than 100 because approximately 16% of victims from Massachusetts reported experiencing more than one type of identity theft.
[2]Includes fraud involving checking and savings accounts and electronic fund transfers.

MICHIGAN

Consumer Sentinel Complaint Figures
January 1 - December 31, 2007

Total Number of Fraud and Identity Theft Consumer Complaints = 21,859

ConsumerSentinel

Fraud Complaints from Michigan Consumers = 14,780

Top Fraud Complaint Categories for Michigan Consumers

Rank	Top Categories	Complaints	Percentage[1]
1	Shop-at-Home/Catalog Sales	1,617	11%
2	Prizes/Sweepstakes and Lotteries	1,040	7%
3	Internet Services	974	7%
4	Foreign Money Offers	775	5%
5	Multi-Level Mktg/Pyramids/Chain Letters	727	5%

[1]Percentages are based on the total number of fraud complaints from Michigan consumers (14,780).

Amount Paid Reported by Michigan Consumers

Total No. of Complaints	Total Amount Paid Reported	Total Complaints Reporting Amt Pd	Percentage of Complaints Reporting Amount Paid	Average Amount Paid[2]
14,780	$18,495,232	12,784	86%	$1,447

[2]Average amount paid is based on the total number of fraud complaints where amount paid was reported by Michigan consumers (12,784). Two consumers reported an amount paid of $1 million or more.

IDENTITY THEFT Data Clearinghouse

Identity Theft Complaints from Michigan Victims = 7,079

Identity Theft Types Reported by Michigan Victims

Rank	Identity Theft Type	Complaints	Percentage[1]
1	Credit Card Fraud	1,772	25%
2	Phone or Utilities Fraud	1,510	21%
3	Government Documents or Benefits Fraud	857	12%
4	Bank Fraud[2]	775	11%
5	Loan Fraud	480	7%
6	Employment-Related Fraud	445	6%
	Other	1,782	25%
	Attempted Identity Theft	458	6%

[1]Percentages are based on the 7,079 victims reporting from Michigan. Percentages add to more than 100 because approximately 17% of victims from Michigan reported experiencing more than one type of identity theft.
[2]Includes fraud involving checking and savings accounts and electronic fund transfers.

MINNESOTA

Consumer Sentinel Complaint Figures
January 1 - December 31, 2007

Total Number of Fraud and Identity Theft Consumer Complaints = 12,245

ConsumerSentinel

Fraud Complaints from Minnesota Consumers = 9,388

Top Fraud Complaint Categories for Minnesota Consumers

Rank	Top Categories	Complaints	Percentage[1]
1	Shop-at-Home/Catalog Sales	915	10%
2	Internet Services	654	7%
3	Foreign Money Offers	490	5%
4	Prizes/Sweepstakes and Lotteries	483	5%
5	Computer Equipment and Software	474	5%

[1]Percentages are based on the total number of fraud complaints from Minnesota consumers (9,388).

Amount Paid Reported by Minnesota Consumers

Total No. of Complaints	Total Amount Paid Reported	Total Complaints Reporting Amt Pd	Percentage of Complaints Reporting Amount Paid	Average Amount Paid[2]
9,388	$8,583,545	8,656	92%	$992

[2]Average amount paid is based on the total number of fraud complaints where amount paid was reported by Minnesota consumers (8,656). One consumer reported an amount paid of $1 million.

IDENTITY THEFT Data Clearinghouse

Identity Theft Complaints from Minnesota Victims = 2,857

Identity Theft Types Reported by Minnesota Victims

Rank	Identity Theft Type	Complaints	Percentage[1]
1	Credit Card Fraud	779	27%
2	Bank Fraud[2]	546	19%
3	Phone or Utilities Fraud	390	14%
4	Employment-Related Fraud	297	10%
5	Government Documents or Benefits Fraud	207	7%
6	Loan Fraud	118	4%
	Other	727	25%
	Attempted Identity Theft	180	6%

[1]Percentages are based on the 2,857 victims reporting from Minnesota. Percentages add to more than 100 because approximately 16% of victims from Minnesota reported experiencing more than one type of identity theft.
[2]Includes fraud involving checking and savings accounts and electronic fund transfers.

MISSISSIPPI

Consumer Sentinel Complaint Figures
January 1 - December 31, 2007

Total Number of Fraud and Identity Theft Consumer Complaints = 4,317

ConsumerSentinel

Fraud Complaints from Mississippi Consumers = 2,644

Top Fraud Complaint Categories for Mississippi Consumers

Rank	Top Categories	Complaints	Percentage[1]
1	Shop-at-Home/Catalog Sales	312	12%
2	Internet Services	212	8%
3	Prizes/Sweepstakes and Lotteries	189	7%
4	Foreign Money Offers	162	6%
5	Advance-Fee Loans and Credit Protection/Repair	130	5%

[1]Percentages are based on the total number of fraud complaints from Mississippi consumers (2,644).

Amount Paid Reported by Mississippi Consumers

Total No. of Complaints	Total Amount Paid Reported	Total Complaints Reporting Amt Pd	Percentage of Complaints Reporting Amount Paid	Average Amount Paid[2]
2,644	$2,679,439	2,406	91%	$1,114

[2]Average amount paid is based on the total number of fraud complaints where amount paid was reported by Mississippi consumers (2,406).

IDENTITY THEFT

Identity Theft Complaints from Mississippi Victims = 1,673

Identity Theft Types Reported by Mississippi Victims

Rank	Identity Theft Type	Complaints	Percentage[1]
1	Government Documents or Benefits Fraud	379	23%
2	Credit Card Fraud	327	20%
3	Phone or Utilities Fraud	288	17%
4	Bank Fraud[2]	204	12%
5	Employment-Related Fraud	142	8%
6	Loan Fraud	76	5%
	Other	417	25%
	Attempted Identity Theft	57	3%

[1]Percentages are based on the 1,673 victims reporting from Mississippi. Percentages add to more than 100 because approximately 15% of victims from Mississippi reported experiencing more than one type of identity theft.

[2]Includes fraud involving checking and savings accounts and electronic fund transfers.

MISSOURI

Consumer Sentinel Complaint Figures
January 1 - December 31, 2007

Total Number of Fraud and Identity Theft Consumer Complaints = 16,874

ConsumerSentinel

Fraud Complaints from Missouri Consumers = 12,912

Top Fraud Complaint Categories for Missouri Consumers

Rank	Top Categories	Complaints	Percentage[1]
1	Shop-at-Home/Catalog Sales	1,214	9%
2	Internet Services	807	6%
3	Foreign Money Offers	624	5%
4	Health Care	619	5%
5	Prizes/Sweepstakes and Lotteries	595	5%

[1]Percentages are based on the total number of fraud complaints from Missouri consumers (12,912).

Amount Paid Reported by Missouri Consumers

Total No. of Complaints	Total Amount Paid Reported	Total Complaints Reporting Amt Pd	Percentage of Complaints Reporting Amount Paid	Average Amount Paid[2]
12,912	$20,758,278	11,979	93%	$1,733

[2]Average amount paid is based on the total number of fraud complaints where amount paid was reported by Missouri consumers (11,979). Two consumers reported an amount paid of $1 million or more.

IDENTITY THEFT Data Clearinghouse

Identity Theft Complaints from Missouri Victims = 3,962

Identity Theft Types Reported by Missouri Victims

Rank	Identity Theft Type	Complaints	Percentage[1]
1	Credit Card Fraud	1,048	26%
2	Phone or Utilities Fraud	681	17%
3	Bank Fraud[2]	619	16%
4	Government Documents or Benefits Fraud	303	8%
5	Employment-Related Fraud	285	7%
6	Loan Fraud	194	5%
	Other	1,084	27%
	Attempted Identity Theft	256	6%

[1]Percentages are based on the 3,962 victims reporting from Missouri. Percentages add to more than 100 because approximately 16% of victims from Missouri reported experiencing more than one type of identity theft.

[2]Includes fraud involving checking and savings accounts and electronic fund transfers.

MONTANA

Consumer Sentinel Complaint Figures
January 1 - December 31, 2007

Total Number of Fraud and Identity Theft Consumer Complaints = 1,887

ConsumerSentinel

Fraud Complaints from Montana Consumers = 1,496

Top Fraud Complaint Categories for Montana Consumers

Rank	Top Categories	Complaints	Percentage[1]
1	Shop-at-Home/Catalog Sales	207	14%
2	Prizes/Sweepstakes and Lotteries	117	8%
3	Internet Services	108	7%
4	Foreign Money Offers	97	6%
5	Internet Auctions	71	5%

[1]Percentages are based on the total number of fraud complaints from Montana consumers (1,496).

Amount Paid Reported by Montana Consumers

Total No. of Complaints	Total Amount Paid Reported	Total Complaints Reporting Amt Pd	Percentage of Complaints Reporting Amount Paid	Average Amount Paid[2]
1,496	$1,298,969	1,338	89%	$971

[2]Average amount paid is based on the total number of fraud complaints where amount paid was reported by Montana consumers (1,338).

IDENTITY THEFT Data Clearinghouse

Identity Theft Complaints from Montana Victims = 391

Identity Theft Types Reported by Montana Victims

Rank	Identity Theft Type	Complaints	Percentage[1]
1	Credit Card Fraud	99	25%
2	Phone or Utilities Fraud	72	18%
3	Bank Fraud[2]	55	14%
4	Employment-Related Fraud	29	7%
5	Government Documents or Benefits Fraud	23	6%
6	Loan Fraud	17	4%
	Other	116	30%
	Attempted Identity Theft	21	5%

[1]Percentages are based on the 391 victims reporting from Montana. Percentages add to more than 100 because approximately 13% of victims from Montana reported experiencing more than one type of identity theft.
[2]Includes fraud involving checking and savings accounts and electronic fund transfers.

NEBRASKA

Consumer Sentinel Complaint Figures
January 1 - December 31, 2007

Total Number of Fraud and Identity Theft Consumer Complaints = 3,624

ConsumerSentinel

Fraud Complaints from Nebraska Consumers = 2,831

Top Fraud Complaint Categories for Nebraska Consumers

Rank	Top Categories	Complaints	Percentage[1]
1	Shop-at-Home/Catalog Sales	310	11%
2	Internet Services	219	8%
3	Prizes/Sweepstakes and Lotteries	158	6%
4	Foreign Money Offers	136	5%
5	Computer Equipment and Software	136	5%

[1]Percentages are based on the total number of fraud complaints from Nebraska consumers (2,831).

Amount Paid Reported by Nebraska Consumers

Total No. of Complaints	Total Amount Paid Reported	Total Complaints Reporting Amt Pd	Percentage of Complaints Reporting Amount Paid	Average Amount Paid[2]
2,831	$2,286,804	2,612	92%	$875

[2]Average amount paid is based on the total number of fraud complaints where amount paid was reported by Nebraska consumers (2,612).

IDENTITY THEFT Data Clearinghouse

Identity Theft Complaints from Nebraska Victims = 793

Identity Theft Types Reported by Nebraska Victims

Rank	Identity Theft Type	Complaints	Percentage[1]
1	Credit Card Fraud	215	27%
2	Employment-Related Fraud	120	15%
3	Bank Fraud[2]	115	15%
4	Phone or Utilities Fraud	102	13%
5	Government Documents or Benefits Fraud	60	8%
6	Loan Fraud	29	4%
	Other	192	24%
	Attempted Identity Theft	44	6%

[1]Percentages are based on the 793 victims reporting from Nebraska. Percentages add to more than 100 because approximately 12% of victims from Nebraska reported experiencing more than one type of identity theft.
[2]Includes fraud involving checking and savings accounts and electronic fund transfers.

NEVADA

Consumer Sentinel Complaint Figures
January 1 - December 31, 2007

Total Number of Fraud and Identity Theft Consumer Complaints = 8,068

ConsumerSentinel

Fraud Complaints from Nevada Consumers = 5,138

Top Fraud Complaint Categories for Nevada Consumers

Rank	Top Categories	Complaints	Percentage[1]
1	Shop-at-Home/Catalog Sales	578	11%
2	Internet Services	393	8%
3	Foreign Money Offers	358	7%
4	Prizes/Sweepstakes and Lotteries	311	6%
5	Internet Auctions	286	6%

[1]Percentages are based on the total number of fraud complaints from Nevada consumers (5,138).

Amount Paid Reported by Nevada Consumers

Total No. of Complaints	Total Amount Paid Reported	Total Complaints Reporting Amt Pd	Percentage of Complaints Reporting Amount Paid	Average Amount Paid[2]
5,138	$12,377,267	4,602	90%	$2,690

[2]Average amount paid is based on the total number of fraud complaints where amount paid was reported by Nevada consumers (4,602). Three consumers reported an amount paid of $1 million or more.

IDENTITY THEFT Data Clearinghouse

Identity Theft Complaints from Nevada Victims = 2,930

Identity Theft Types Reported by Nevada Victims

Rank	Identity Theft Type	Complaints	Percentage[1]
1	Credit Card Fraud	702	24%
2	Phone or Utilities Fraud	491	17%
3	Employment-Related Fraud	462	16%
4	Bank Fraud[2]	432	15%
5	Government Documents or Benefits Fraud	218	7%
6	Loan Fraud	185	6%
	Other	790	27%
	Attempted Identity Theft	148	5%

[1]Percentages are based on the 2,930 victims reporting from Nevada. Percentages add to more than 100 because approximately 18% of victims from Nevada reported experiencing more than one type of identity theft.

[2]Includes fraud involving checking and savings accounts and electronic fund transfers.

NEW HAMPSHIRE

Consumer Sentinel Complaint Figures
January 1 - December 31, 2007

Total Number of Fraud and Identity Theft Consumer Complaints = 3,345

ConsumerSentinel

Fraud Complaints from New Hampshire Consumers = 2,702

Top Fraud Complaint Categories for New Hampshire Consumers

Rank	Top Categories	Complaints	Percentage[1]
1	Shop-at-Home/Catalog Sales	336	12%
2	Internet Services	205	8%
3	Foreign Money Offers	190	7%
4	Prizes/Sweepstakes and Lotteries	182	7%
5	Internet Auctions	130	5%

[1]Percentages are based on the total number of fraud complaints from New Hampshire consumers (2,702).

Amount Paid Reported by New Hampshire Consumers

Total No. of Complaints	Total Amount Paid Reported	Total Complaints Reporting Amt Pd	Percentage of Complaints Reporting Amount Paid	Average Amount Paid[2]
2,702	$2,930,542	2,433	90%	$1,204

[2]Average amount paid is based on the total number of fraud complaints where amount paid was reported by New Hampshire consumers (2,433). One consumer reported an amount paid of $1.3 million.

IDENTITY THEFT Data Clearinghouse

Identity Theft Complaints from New Hampshire Victims = 643

Identity Theft Types Reported by New Hampshire Victims

Rank	Identity Theft Type	Complaints	Percentage[1]
1	Credit Card Fraud	186	29%
2	Phone or Utilities Fraud	103	16%
3	Bank Fraud[2]	73	11%
4	Employment-Related Fraud	37	6%
5	Government Documents or Benefits Fraud	35	5%
6	Loan Fraud	32	5%
	Other	216	34%
	Attempted Identity Theft	47	7%

[1]Percentages are based on the 643 victims reporting from New Hampshire. Percentages add to more than 100 because approximately 16% of victims from New Hampshire reported experiencing more than one type of identity theft.
[2]Includes fraud involving checking and savings accounts and electronic fund transfers.

NEW JERSEY

Consumer Sentinel Complaint Figures
January 1 - December 31, 2007

Total Number of Fraud and Identity Theft Consumer Complaints = 21,406

ConsumerSentinel

Fraud Complaints from New Jersey Consumers = 14,542

Top Fraud Complaint Categories for New Jersey Consumers

Rank	Top Categories	Complaints	Percentage[1]
1	Shop-at-Home/Catalog Sales	1,772	12%
2	Internet Services	1,202	8%
3	Computer Equipment and Software	884	6%
4	Foreign Money Offers	807	6%
5	Prizes/Sweepstakes and Lotteries	766	5%

[1]Percentages are based on the total number of fraud complaints from New Jersey consumers (14,542).

Amount Paid Reported by New Jersey Consumers

Total No. of Complaints	Total Amount Paid Reported	Total Complaints Reporting Amt Pd	Percentage of Complaints Reporting Amount Paid	Average Amount Paid[2]
14,542	$32,325,378	13,199	91%	$2,449

[2]Average amount paid is based on the total number of fraud complaints where amount paid was reported by New Jersey consumers (13,199). One consumer reported an amount paid of $2 million.

IDENTITY THEFT Data Clearinghouse

Identity Theft Complaints from New Jersey Victims = 6,864

Identity Theft Types Reported by New Jersey Victims

Rank	Identity Theft Type	Complaints	Percentage[1]
1	Credit Card Fraud	1,909	28%
2	Phone or Utilities Fraud	1,291	19%
3	Bank Fraud[2]	818	12%
4	Employment-Related Fraud	687	10%
5	Government Documents or Benefits Fraud	624	9%
6	Loan Fraud	305	4%
	Other	1,765	26%
	Attempted Identity Theft	408	6%

[1]Percentages are based on the 6,864 victims reporting from New Jersey. Percentages add to more than 100 because approximately 15% of victims from New Jersey reported experiencing more than one type of identity theft.
[2]Includes fraud involving checking and savings accounts and electronic fund transfers.

NEW MEXICO

Consumer Sentinel Complaint Figures
January 1 - December 31, 2007

Total Number of Fraud and Identity Theft Consumer Complaints = 4,420

ConsumerSentinel

Fraud Complaints from New Mexico Consumers = 2,697

Top Fraud Complaint Categories for New Mexico Consumers

Rank	Top Categories	Complaints	Percentage[1]
1	Shop-at-Home/Catalog Sales	307	11%
2	Internet Services	221	8%
3	Prizes/Sweepstakes and Lotteries	186	7%
4	Foreign Money Offers	158	6%
5	Computer Equipment and Software	114	4%

[1]Percentages are based on the total number of fraud complaints from New Mexico consumers (2,697).

Amount Paid Reported by New Mexico Consumers

Total No. of Complaints	Total Amount Paid Reported	Total Complaints Reporting Amt Pd	Percentage of Complaints Reporting Amount Paid	Average Amount Paid[2]
2,697	$4,259,902	2,423	90%	$1,758

[2]Average amount paid is based on the total number of fraud complaints where amount paid was reported by New Mexico consumers (2,423). One consumer reported an amount paid of $1 million.

IDENTITY THEFT Data Clearinghouse

Identity Theft Complaints from New Mexico Victims = 1,723

Identity Theft Types Reported by New Mexico Victims

Rank	Identity Theft Type	Complaints	Percentage[1]
1	Employment-Related Fraud	353	20%
2	Credit Card Fraud	350	20%
3	Bank Fraud[2]	253	15%
4	Phone or Utilities Fraud	194	11%
5	Government Documents or Benefits Fraud	163	9%
6	Loan Fraud	84	5%
	Other	518	30%
	Attempted Identity Theft	85	5%

[1]Percentages are based on the 1,723 victims reporting from New Mexico. Percentages add to more than 100 because approximately 17% of victims from New Mexico reported experiencing more than one type of identity theft.
[2]Includes fraud involving checking and savings accounts and electronic fund transfers.

NEW YORK

Consumer Sentinel Complaint Figures
January 1 - December 31, 2007

Total Number of Fraud and Identity Theft Consumer Complaints = 46,538

ConsumerSentinel

Fraud Complaints from New York Consumers = 27,219

Top Fraud Complaint Categories for New York Consumers

Rank	Top Categories	Complaints	Percentage[1]
1	Shop-at-Home/Catalog Sales	3,785	14%
2	Internet Services	2,332	9%
3	Foreign Money Offers	1,720	6%
4	Computer Equipment and Software	1,676	6%
5	Internet Auctions	1,659	6%

[1]Percentages are based on the total number of fraud complaints from New York consumers (27,219).

Amount Paid Reported by New York Consumers

Total No. of Complaints	Total Amount Paid Reported	Total Complaints Reporting Amt Pd	Percentage of Complaints Reporting Amount Paid	Average Amount Paid[2]
27,219	$46,103,842	24,329	89%	$1,895

[2]Average amount paid is based on the total number of fraud complaints where amount paid was reported by New York consumers (24,329). Nine consumers reported an amount paid of $1 million or more.

IDENTITY THEFT Data Clearinghouse

Identity Theft Complaints from New York Victims = 19,319

Identity Theft Types Reported by New York Victims

Rank	Identity Theft Type	Complaints	Percentage[1]
1	Phone or Utilities Fraud	5,404	28%
2	Credit Card Fraud	4,934	26%
3	Government Documents or Benefits Fraud	2,096	11%
4	Bank Fraud[2]	1,942	10%
5	Employment-Related Fraud	1,371	7%
6	Loan Fraud	901	5%
	Other	4,078	21%
	Attempted Identity Theft	1,035	5%

[1]Percentages are based on the 19,319 victims reporting from New York. Percentages add to more than 100 because approximately 15% of victims from New York reported experiencing more than one type of identity theft.
[2]Includes fraud involving checking and savings accounts and electronic fund transfers.

NORTH CAROLINA

Consumer Sentinel Complaint Figures
January 1 - December 31, 2007

Total Number of Fraud and Identity Theft Consumer Complaints = 20,915

ConsumerSentinel

Fraud Complaints from North Carolina Consumers = 14,846

Top Fraud Complaint Categories for North Carolina Consumers

Rank	Top Categories	Complaints	Percentage[1]
1	Shop-at-Home/Catalog Sales	1,496	10%
2	Internet Services	1,104	7%
3	Foreign Money Offers	801	5%
4	Computer Equipment and Software	765	5%
5	Prizes/Sweepstakes and Lotteries	758	5%

[1]Percentages are based on the total number of fraud complaints from North Carolina consumers (14,846).

Amount Paid Reported by North Carolina Consumers

Total No. of Complaints	Total Amount Paid Reported	Total Complaints Reporting Amt Pd	Percentage of Complaints Reporting Amount Paid	Average Amount Paid[2]
14,846	$20,816,318	13,607	92%	$1,530

[2]Average amount paid is based on the total number of fraud complaints where amount paid was reported by North Carolina consumers (13,607). Four consumers reported an amount paid of $1 million or more.

IDENTITY THEFT Data Clearinghouse

Identity Theft Complaints from North Carolina Victims = 6,069

Identity Theft Types Reported by North Carolina Victims

Rank	Identity Theft Type	Complaints	Percentage[1]
1	Credit Card Fraud	1,284	21%
2	Phone or Utilities Fraud	1,184	20%
3	Bank Fraud[2]	819	13%
4	Government Documents or Benefits Fraud	717	12%
5	Employment-Related Fraud	687	11%
6	Loan Fraud	307	5%
	Other	1,557	26%
	Attempted Identity Theft	321	5%

[1]Percentages are based on the 6,069 victims reporting from North Carolina. Percentages add to more than 100 because approximately 16% of victims from North Carolina reported experiencing more than one type of identity theft.
[2]Includes fraud involving checking and savings accounts and electronic fund transfers.

NORTH DAKOTA

Consumer Sentinel Complaint Figures
January 1 - December 31, 2007

Total Number of Fraud and Identity Theft Consumer Complaints = 908

ConsumerSentinel

Fraud Complaints from North Dakota Consumers = 726

Top Fraud Complaint Categories for North Dakota Consumers

Rank	Top Categories	Complaints	Percentage[1]
1	Shop-at-Home/Catalog Sales	87	12%
2	Internet Auctions	56	8%
3	Foreign Money Offers	38	5%
4	Internet Services	36	5%
5	Advance-Fee Loans and Credit Protection/Repair	31	4%
6	Computer Equipment and Software	31	4%

[1]Percentages are based on the total number of fraud complaints from North Dakota consumers (726).

Amount Paid Reported by North Dakota Consumers

Total No. of Complaints	Total Amount Paid Reported	Total Complaints Reporting Amt Pd	Percentage of Complaints Reporting Amount Paid	Average Amount Paid[2]
726	$540,446	660	91%	$819

[2]Average amount paid is based on the total number of fraud complaints where amount paid was reported by North Dakota consumers (660).

IDENTITY THEFT Data Clearinghouse

Identity Theft Complaints from North Dakota Victims = 182

Identity Theft Types Reported by North Dakota Victims

Rank	Identity Theft Type	Complaints	Percentage[1]
1	Credit Card Fraud	46	25%
2	Phone or Utilities Fraud	32	18%
3	Bank Fraud[2]	21	12%
4	Employment-Related Fraud	16	9%
5	Government Documents or Benefits Fraud	13	7%
6	Loan Fraud	7	4%
	Other	56	31%
	Attempted Identity Theft	13	7%

[1]Percentages are based on the 182 victims reporting from North Dakota. Percentages add to more than 100 because approximately 14% of victims from North Dakota reported experiencing more than one type of identity theft.
[2]Includes fraud involving checking and savings accounts and electronic fund transfers.

OHIO

Consumer Sentinel Complaint Figures
January 1 - December 31, 2007

Total Number of Fraud and Identity Theft Consumer Complaints = 26,142

ConsumerSentinel

Fraud Complaints from Ohio Consumers = 18,964

Top Fraud Complaint Categories for Ohio Consumers

Rank	Top Categories	Complaints	Percentage[1]
1	Shop-at-Home/Catalog Sales	2,213	12%
2	Internet Services	1,274	7%
3	Prizes/Sweepstakes and Lotteries	1,135	6%
4	Computer Equipment and Software	1,028	5%
5	Foreign Money Offers	885	5%

[1]Percentages are based on the total number of fraud complaints from Ohio consumers (18,964).

Amount Paid Reported by Ohio Consumers

Total No. of Complaints	Total Amount Paid Reported	Total Complaints Reporting Amt Pd	Percentage of Complaints Reporting Amount Paid	Average Amount Paid[2]
18,964	$19,324,015	17,318	91%	$1,116

[2]Average amount paid is based on the total number of fraud complaints where amount paid was reported by Ohio consumers (17,318). Three consumers reported an amount paid of $1 million or more.

IDENTITY THEFT Data Clearinghouse

Identity Theft Complaints from Ohio Victims = 7,178

Identity Theft Types Reported by Ohio Victims

Rank	Identity Theft Type	Complaints	Percentage[1]
1	Phone or Utilities Fraud	2,034	28%
2	Credit Card Fraud	1,631	23%
3	Bank Fraud[2]	889	12%
4	Government Documents or Benefits Fraud	692	10%
5	Employment-Related Fraud	406	6%
6	Loan Fraud	281	4%
	Other	1,753	24%
	Attempted Identity Theft	410	6%

[1]Percentages are based on the 7,178 victims reporting from Ohio. Percentages add to more than 100 because approximately 15% of victims from Ohio reported experiencing more than one type of identity theft.
[2]Includes fraud involving checking and savings accounts and electronic fund transfers.

OKLAHOMA

Consumer Sentinel Complaint Figures
January 1 - December 31, 2007

Total Number of Fraud and Identity Theft Consumer Complaints = 7,140

Fraud Complaints from Oklahoma Consumers = 4,828

Top Fraud Complaint Categories for Oklahoma Consumers

Rank	Top Categories	Complaints	Percentage[1]
1	Shop-at-Home/Catalog Sales	501	10%
2	Internet Services	350	7%
3	Prizes/Sweepstakes and Lotteries	281	6%
4	Foreign Money Offers	241	5%
5	Computer Equipment and Software	237	5%

[1]Percentages are based on the total number of fraud complaints from Oklahoma consumers (4,828).

Amount Paid Reported by Oklahoma Consumers

Total No. of Complaints	Total Amount Paid Reported	Total Complaints Reporting Amt Pd	Percentage of Complaints Reporting Amount Paid	Average Amount Paid[2]
4,828	$5,711,975	4,401	91%	$1,298

[2]Average amount paid is based on the total number of fraud complaints where amount paid was reported by Oklahoma consumers (4,401). Two consumers reported an amount paid of $1 million or more.

Identity Theft Complaints from Oklahoma Victims = 2,312

Identity Theft Types Reported by Oklahoma Victims

Rank	Identity Theft Type	Complaints	Percentage[1]
1	Credit Card Fraud	538	23%
2	Phone or Utilities Fraud	412	18%
3	Bank Fraud[2]	358	15%
4	Government Documents or Benefits Fraud	303	13%
5	Employment-Related Fraud	242	10%
6	Loan Fraud	105	5%
	Other	553	24%
	Attempted Identity Theft	116	5%

[1]Percentages are based on the 2,312 victims reporting from Oklahoma. Percentages add to more than 100 because approximately 15% of victims from Oklahoma reported experiencing more than one type of identity theft.
[2]Includes fraud involving checking and savings accounts and electronic fund transfers.

OREGON

Consumer Sentinel Complaint Figures
January 1 - December 31, 2007

Total Number of Fraud and Identity Theft Consumer Complaints = 10,256

Fraud Complaints from Oregon Consumers = 7,704

Top Fraud Complaint Categories for Oregon Consumers

Rank	Top Categories	Complaints	Percentage[1]
1	Shop-at-Home/Catalog Sales	753	10%
2	Internet Services	671	9%
3	Foreign Money Offers	551	7%
4	Computer Equipment and Software	374	5%
5	Internet Auctions	330	4%

[1]Percentages are based on the total number of fraud complaints from Oregon consumers (7,704).

Amount Paid Reported by Oregon Consumers

Total No. of Complaints	Total Amount Paid Reported	Total Complaints Reporting Amt Pd	Percentage of Complaints Reporting Amount Paid	Average Amount Paid[2]
7,704	$10,258,965	6,931	90%	$1,480

[2]Average amount paid is based on the total number of fraud complaints where amount paid was reported by Oregon consumers (6,931). Three consumers reported an amount paid of $1 million or more.

Identity Theft Complaints from Oregon Victims = 2,552

Identity Theft Types Reported by Oregon Victims

Rank	Identity Theft Type	Complaints	Percentage[1]
1	Credit Card Fraud	591	23%
2	Bank Fraud[2]	433	17%
3	Phone or Utilities Fraud	399	16%
4	Employment-Related Fraud	236	9%
5	Government Documents or Benefits Fraud	136	5%
6	Loan Fraud	118	5%
	Other	766	30%
	Attempted Identity Theft	152	6%

[1]Percentages are based on the 2,552 victims reporting from Oregon. Percentages add to more than 100 because approximately 14% of victims from Oregon reported experiencing more than one type of identity theft.
[2]Includes fraud involving checking and savings accounts and electronic fund transfers.

PENNSYLVANIA

Consumer Sentinel Complaint Figures
January 1 - December 31, 2007

Total Number of Fraud and Identity Theft Consumer Complaints = 28,213

ConsumerSentinel

Fraud Complaints from Pennsylvania Consumers = 19,197

Top Fraud Complaint Categories for Pennsylvania Consumers

Rank	Top Categories	Complaints	Percentage[1]
1	Shop-at-Home/Catalog Sales	2,505	13%
2	Prizes/Sweepstakes and Lotteries	1,599	8%
3	Internet Services	1,419	7%
4	Computer Equipment and Software	1,153	6%
5	Foreign Money Offers	1,032	5%

[1]Percentages are based on the total number of fraud complaints from Pennsylvania consumers (19,197).

Amount Paid Reported by Pennsylvania Consumers

Total No. of Complaints	Total Amount Paid Reported	Total Complaints Reporting Amt Pd	Percentage of Complaints Reporting Amount Paid	Average Amount Paid[2]
19,197	$32,166,694	17,179	89%	$1,872

[2]Average amount paid is based on the total number of fraud complaints where amount paid was reported by Pennsylvania consumers (17,179). Three consumers reported an amount paid of $1 million or more.

IDENTITY THEFT Data Clearinghouse

Identity Theft Complaints from Pennsylvania Victims = 9,016

Identity Theft Types Reported by Pennsylvania Victims

Rank	Identity Theft Type	Complaints	Percentage[1]
1	Credit Card Fraud	2,424	27%
2	Phone or Utilities Fraud	2,106	23%
3	Bank Fraud[2]	1,125	12%
4	Government Documents or Benefits Fraud	848	9%
5	Employment-Related Fraud	576	6%
6	Loan Fraud	400	4%
	Other	2,146	24%
	Attempted Identity Theft	521	6%

[1]Percentages are based on the 9,016 victims reporting from Pennsylvania. Percentages add to more than 100 because approximately 15% of victims from Pennsylvania reported experiencing more than one type of identity theft.
[2]Includes fraud involving checking and savings accounts and electronic fund transfers.

RHODE ISLAND

Consumer Sentinel Complaint Figures
January 1 - December 31, 2007

Total Number of Fraud and Identity Theft Consumer Complaints = 2,103

ConsumerSentinel

Fraud Complaints from Rhode Island Consumers = 1,511

Top Fraud Complaint Categories for Rhode Island Consumers

Rank	Top Categories	Complaints	Percentage[1]
1	Shop-at-Home/Catalog Sales	192	13%
2	Computer Equipment and Software	102	7%
3	Internet Services	101	7%
4	Prizes/Sweepstakes and Lotteries	89	6%
5	Foreign Money Offers	83	5%

[1]Percentages are based on the total number of fraud complaints from Rhode Island consumers (1,511).

Amount Paid Reported by Rhode Island Consumers

Total No. of Complaints	Total Amount Paid Reported	Total Complaints Reporting Amt Pd	Percentage of Complaints Reporting Amount Paid	Average Amount Paid[2]
1,511	$2,402,431	1,361	90%	$1,765

[2]Average amount paid is based on the total number of fraud complaints where amount paid was reported by Rhode Island consumers (1,361).

IDENTITY THEFT Data Clearinghouse

Identity Theft Complaints from Rhode Island Victims = 592

Identity Theft Types Reported by Rhode Island Victims

Rank	Identity Theft Type	Complaints	Percentage[1]
1	Credit Card Fraud	172	29%
2	Phone or Utilities Fraud	108	18%
3	Bank Fraud[2]	79	13%
4	Employment-Related Fraud	63	11%
5	Government Documents or Benefits Fraud	51	9%
6	Loan Fraud	28	5%
	Other	140	24%
	Attempted Identity Theft	39	7%

[1]Percentages are based on the 592 victims reporting from Rhode Island. Percentages add to more than 100 because approximately 18% of victims from Rhode Island reported experiencing more than one type of identity theft.
[2]Includes fraud involving checking and savings accounts and electronic fund transfers.

SOUTH CAROLINA

Consumer Sentinel Complaint Figures
January 1 - December 31, 2007

Total Number of Fraud and Identity Theft Consumer Complaints = 8,711

Consumer Sentinel

Fraud Complaints from South Carolina Consumers = 6,041

Top Fraud Complaint Categories for South Carolina Consumers

Rank	Top Categories	Complaints	Percentage[1]
1	Shop-at-Home/Catalog Sales	615	10%
2	Foreign Money Offers	465	8%
3	Internet Services	439	7%
4	Prizes/Sweepstakes and Lotteries	377	6%
5	Computer Equipment and Software	374	6%

[1]Percentages are based on the total number of fraud complaints from South Carolina consumers (6,041).

Amount Paid Reported by South Carolina Consumers

Total No. of Complaints	Total Amount Paid Reported	Total Complaints Reporting Amt Pd	Percentage of Complaints Reporting Amount Paid	Average Amount Paid[2]
6,041	$9,064,886	5,508	91%	$1,646

[2]Average amount paid is based on the total number of fraud complaints where amount paid was reported by South Carolina consumers (5,508). One consumer reported an amount paid of $2 million.

IDENTITY THEFT Data Clearinghouse

Identity Theft Complaints from South Carolina Victims = 2,670

Identity Theft Types Reported by South Carolina Victims

Rank	Identity Theft Type	Complaints	Percentage[1]
1	Credit Card Fraud	563	21%
2	Phone or Utilities Fraud	495	19%
3	Bank Fraud[2]	404	15%
4	Government Documents or Benefits Fraud	369	14%
5	Employment-Related Fraud	256	10%
6	Loan Fraud	125	5%
	Other	701	26%
	Attempted Identity Theft	115	4%

[1]Percentages are based on the 2,670 victims reporting from South Carolina. Percentages add to more than 100 because approximately 16% of victims from South Carolina reported experiencing more than one type of identity theft.
[2]Includes fraud involving checking and savings accounts and electronic fund transfers.

SOUTH DAKOTA

Consumer Sentinel Complaint Figures
January 1 - December 31, 2007

Total Number of Fraud and Identity Theft Consumer Complaints = 1,125

ConsumerSentinel

Fraud Complaints from South Dakota Consumers = 880

Top Fraud Complaint Categories for South Dakota Consumers

Rank	Top Categories	Complaints	Percentage[1]
1	Shop-at-Home/Catalog Sales	108	12%
2	Prizes/Sweepstakes and Lotteries	75	9%
3	Internet Services	62	7%
4	Internet Auctions	51	6%
5	Foreign Money Offers	45	5%

[1]Percentages are based on the total number of fraud complaints from South Dakota consumers (880).

Amount Paid Reported by South Dakota Consumers

Total No. of Complaints	Total Amount Paid Reported	Total Complaints Reporting Amt Pd	Percentage of Complaints Reporting Amount Paid	Average Amount Paid[2]
880	$916,320	781	89%	$1,173

[2]Average amount paid is based on the total number of fraud complaints where amount paid was reported by South Dakota consumers (781).

IDENTITY THEFT Data Clearinghouse

Identity Theft Complaints from South Dakota Victims = 245

Identity Theft Types Reported by South Dakota Victims

Rank	Identity Theft Type	Complaints	Percentage[1]
1	Credit Card Fraud	78	32%
2	Phone or Utilities Fraud	35	14%
3	Bank Fraud[2]	34	14%
4	Employment-Related Fraud	22	9%
5	Government Documents or Benefits Fraud	14	6%
6	Loan Fraud	10	4%
	Other	62	25%
	Attempted Identity Theft	23	9%

[1]Percentages are based on the 245 victims reporting from South Dakota. Percentages add to more than 100 because approximately 17% of victims from South Dakota reported experiencing more than one type of identity theft.
[2]Includes fraud involving checking and savings accounts and electronic fund transfers.

TENNESSEE

Consumer Sentinel Complaint Figures
January 1 - December 31, 2007

Total Number of Fraud and Identity Theft Consumer Complaints = 13,906

Fraud Complaints from Tennessee Consumers = 9,920

Top Fraud Complaint Categories for Tennessee Consumers

Rank	Top Categories	Complaints	Percentage[1]
1	Shop-at-Home/Catalog Sales	1,139	11%
2	Internet Services	691	7%
3	Prizes/Sweepstakes and Lotteries	564	6%
4	Foreign Money Offers	486	5%
5	Internet Auctions	466	5%

[1]Percentages are based on the total number of fraud complaints from Tennessee consumers (9,920).

Amount Paid Reported by Tennessee Consumers

Total No. of Complaints	Total Amount Paid Reported	Total Complaints Reporting Amt Pd	Percentage of Complaints Reporting Amount Paid	Average Amount Paid[2]
9,920	$13,787,117	9,067	91%	$1,521

[2]Average amount paid is based on the total number of fraud complaints where amount paid was reported by Tennessee consumers (9,067). Three consumers reported an amount paid of $1 million or more.

Identity Theft Complaints from Tennessee Victims = 3,986

Identity Theft Types Reported by Tennessee Victims

Rank	Identity Theft Type	Complaints	Percentage[1]
1	Credit Card Fraud	902	23%
2	Phone or Utilities Fraud	629	16%
3	Government Documents or Benefits Fraud	617	15%
4	Bank Fraud[2]	596	15%
5	Employment-Related Fraud	301	8%
6	Loan Fraud	209	5%
	Other	1,057	27%
	Attempted Identity Theft	217	5%

[1]Percentages are based on the 3,986 victims reporting from Tennessee. Percentages add to more than 100 because approximately 16% of victims from Tennessee reported experiencing more than one type of identity theft.

[2]Includes fraud involving checking and savings accounts and electronic fund transfers.

TEXAS

Consumer Sentinel Complaint Figures
January 1 - December 31, 2007

Total Number of Fraud and Identity Theft Consumer Complaints = 62,163

ConsumerSentinel

Fraud Complaints from Texas Consumers = 36,367

Top Fraud Complaint Categories for Texas Consumers

Rank	Top Categories	Complaints	Percentage[1]
1	Shop-at-Home/Catalog Sales	3,431	9%
2	Internet Services	2,785	8%
3	Foreign Money Offers	2,009	6%
4	Computer Equipment and Software	1,795	5%
5	Prizes/Sweepstakes and Lotteries	1,580	4%

[1]Percentages are based on the total number of fraud complaints from Texas consumers (36,367).

Amount Paid Reported by Texas Consumers

Total No. of Complaints	Total Amount Paid Reported	Total Complaints Reporting Amt Pd	Percentage of Complaints Reporting Amount Paid	Average Amount Paid[2]
36,367	$105,343,306	33,160	91%	$3,177

[2]Average amount paid is based on the total number of fraud complaints where amount paid was reported by Texas consumers (33,160). Fifteen consumers reported an amount paid of $1 million or more.

IDENTITY THEFT Data Clearinghouse

Identity Theft Complaints from Texas Victims = 25,796

Identity Theft Types Reported by Texas Victims

Rank	Identity Theft Type	Complaints	Percentage[1]
1	Employment-Related Fraud	6,312	24%
2	Credit Card Fraud	4,788	19%
3	Bank Fraud[2]	3,836	15%
4	Phone or Utilities Fraud	3,467	13%
5	Government Documents or Benefits Fraud	3,351	13%
6	Loan Fraud	1,515	6%
	Other	5,582	22%
	Attempted Identity Theft	990	4%

[1]Percentages are based on the 25,796 victims reporting from Texas. Percentages add to more than 100 because approximately 17% of victims from Texas reported experiencing more than one type of identity theft.
[2]Includes fraud involving checking and savings accounts and electronic fund transfers.

UTAH

Consumer Sentinel Complaint Figures
January 1 - December 31, 2007

Total Number of Fraud and Identity Theft Consumer Complaints = 6,639

ConsumerSentinel

Fraud Complaints from Utah Consumers = 5,110

Top Fraud Complaint Categories for Utah Consumers

Rank	Top Categories	Complaints	Percentage[1]
1	Shop-at-Home/Catalog Sales	463	9%
2	Internet Services	409	8%
3	Prizes/Sweepstakes and Lotteries	323	6%
4	Foreign Money Offers	283	6%
5	Health Care	248	5%

[1]Percentages are based on the total number of fraud complaints from Utah consumers (5,110).

Amount Paid Reported by Utah Consumers

Total No. of Complaints	Total Amount Paid Reported	Total Complaints Reporting Amt Pd	Percentage of Complaints Reporting Amount Paid	Average Amount Paid[2]
5,110	$8,078,840	4,594	90%	$1,759

[2]Average amount paid is based on the total number of fraud complaints where amount paid was reported by Utah consumers (4,594). One consumer reported an amount paid of $4 million.

IDENTITY THEFT Data Clearinghouse

Identity Theft Complaints from Utah Victims = 1,529

Identity Theft Types Reported by Utah Victims

Rank	Identity Theft Type	Complaints	Percentage[1]
1	Credit Card Fraud	368	24%
2	Bank Fraud[2]	268	18%
3	Phone or Utilities Fraud	203	13%
4	Employment-Related Fraud	199	13%
5	Government Documents or Benefits Fraud	85	6%
6	Loan Fraud	68	4%
	Other	455	30%
	Attempted Identity Theft	84	5%

[1]Percentages are based on the 1,529 victims reporting from Utah. Percentages add to more than 100 because approximately 16% of victims from Utah reported experiencing more than one type of identity theft.

[2]Includes fraud involving checking and savings accounts and electronic fund transfers.

VERMONT

Consumer Sentinel Complaint Figures
January 1 - December 31, 2007

Total Number of Fraud and Identity Theft Consumer Complaints = 1,117

ConsumerSentinel

Fraud Complaints from Vermont Consumers = 880

Top Fraud Complaint Categories for Vermont Consumers

Rank	Top Categories	Complaints	Percentage[1]
1	Shop-at-Home/Catalog Sales	116	13%
2	Internet Services	78	9%
3	Foreign Money Offers	51	6%
4	Internet Auctions	51	6%
5	Prizes/Sweepstakes and Lotteries	43	5%

[1]Percentages are based on the total number of fraud complaints from Vermont consumers (880).

Amount Paid Reported by Vermont Consumers

Total No. of Complaints	Total Amount Paid Reported	Total Complaints Reporting Amt Pd	Percentage of Complaints Reporting Amount Paid	Average Amount Paid[2]
880	$2,516,428	798	91%	$3,153

[2]Average amount paid is based on the total number of fraud complaints where amount paid was reported by Vermont consumers (798). One consumer reported an amount paid of $2 million.

IDENTITY THEFT Data Clearinghouse

Identity Theft Complaints from Vermont Victims = 237

Identity Theft Types Reported by Vermont Victims

Rank	Identity Theft Type	Complaints	Percentage[1]
1	Credit Card Fraud	68	29%
2	Phone or Utilities Fraud	45	19%
3	Bank Fraud[2]	23	10%
4	Government Documents or Benefits Fraud	13	5%
5	Loan Fraud	10	4%
6	Employment-Related Fraud	7	3%
	Other	82	35%
	Attempted Identity Theft	10	4%

[1]Percentages are based on the 237 victims reporting from Vermont. Percentages add to more than 100 because approximately 14% of victims from Vermont reported experiencing more than one type of identity theft.
[2]Includes fraud involving checking and savings accounts and electronic fund transfers.

VIRGINIA

Consumer Sentinel Complaint Figures
January 1 - December 31, 2007

Total Number of Fraud and Identity Theft Consumer Complaints = 20,052

ConsumerSentinel

Fraud Complaints from Virginia Consumers = 14,733

Top Fraud Complaint Categories for Virginia Consumers

Rank	Top Categories	Complaints	Percentage[1]
1	Shop-at-Home/Catalog Sales	1,855	13%
2	Internet Services	1,116	8%
3	Foreign Money Offers	957	6%
4	Prizes/Sweepstakes and Lotteries	873	6%
5	Computer Equipment and Software	775	5%

[1]Percentages are based on the total number of fraud complaints from Virginia consumers (14,733).

Amount Paid Reported by Virginia Consumers

Total No. of Complaints	Total Amount Paid Reported	Total Complaints Reporting Amt Pd	Percentage of Complaints Reporting Amount Paid	Average Amount Paid[2]
14,733	$16,593,111	13,068	89%	$1,270

[2]Average amount paid is based on the total number of fraud complaints where amount paid was reported by Virginia consumers (13,068). Three consumers reported an amount paid of $1 million or more.

IDENTITY THEFT Data Clearinghouse

Identity Theft Complaints from Virginia Victims = 5,319

Identity Theft Types Reported by Virginia Victims

Rank	Identity Theft Type	Complaints	Percentage[1]
1	Credit Card Fraud	1,394	26%
2	Phone or Utilities Fraud	1,222	23%
3	Bank Fraud[2]	685	13%
4	Government Documents or Benefits Fraud	382	7%
5	Employment-Related Fraud	367	7%
6	Loan Fraud	250	5%
	Other	1,433	27%
	Attempted Identity Theft	300	6%

[1]Percentages are based on the 5,319 victims reporting from Virginia. Percentages add to more than 100 because approximately 16% of victims from Virginia reported experiencing more than one type of identity theft.
[2]Includes fraud involving checking and savings accounts and electronic fund transfers.

WASHINGTON

Consumer Sentinel Complaint Figures
January 1 - December 31, 2007

Total Number of Fraud and Identity Theft Consumer Complaints = 19,860

ConsumerSentinel

Fraud Complaints from Washington Consumers = 14,918

Top Fraud Complaint Categories for Washington Consumers

Rank	Top Categories	Complaints	Percentage[1]
1	Shop-at-Home/Catalog Sales	1,404	9%
2	Internet Services	1,226	8%
3	Foreign Money Offers	893	6%
4	Computer Equipment and Software	795	5%
5	Prizes/Sweepstakes and Lotteries	773	5%

[1]Percentages are based on the total number of fraud complaints from Washington consumers (14,918).

Amount Paid Reported by Washington Consumers

Total No. of Complaints	Total Amount Paid Reported	Total Complaints Reporting Amt Pd	Percentage of Complaints Reporting Amount Paid	Average Amount Paid[2]
14,918	$39,417,630	13,478	90%	$2,925

[2]Average amount paid is based on the total number of fraud complaints where amount paid was reported by Washington consumers (13,478). Eleven consumers reported an amount paid of $1 million or more.

IDENTITY THEFT Data Clearinghouse

Identity Theft Complaints from Washington Victims = 4,942

Identity Theft Types Reported by Washington Victims

Rank	Identity Theft Type	Complaints	Percentage[1]
1	Credit Card Fraud	1,174	24%
2	Bank Fraud[2]	951	19%
3	Phone or Utilities Fraud	813	16%
4	Employment-Related Fraud	502	10%
5	Government Documents or Benefits Fraud	304	6%
6	Loan Fraud	197	4%
	Other	1,414	29%
	Attempted Identity Theft	280	6%

[1]Percentages are based on the 4,942 victims reporting from Washington. Percentages add to more than 100 because approximately 16% of victims from Washington reported experiencing more than one type of identity theft.
[2]Includes fraud involving checking and savings accounts and electronic fund transfers.

WEST VIRGINIA

Consumer Sentinel Complaint Figures
January 1 - December 31, 2007

Total Number of Fraud and Identity Theft Consumer Complaints = 3,383

ConsumerSentinel

Fraud Complaints from West Virginia Consumers = 2,654

Top Fraud Complaint Categories for West Virginia Consumers

Rank	Top Categories	Complaints	Percentage[1]
1	Internet Services	420	16%
2	Shop-at-Home/Catalog Sales	357	13%
3	Prizes/Sweepstakes and Lotteries	162	6%
4	Internet Auctions	128	5%
5	Foreign Money Offers	111	4%

[1]Percentages are based on the total number of fraud complaints from West Virginia consumers (2,654).

Amount Paid Reported by West Virginia Consumers

Total No. of Complaints	Total Amount Paid Reported	Total Complaints Reporting Amt Pd	Percentage of Complaints Reporting Amount Paid	Average Amount Paid[2]
2,654	$1,823,592	2,137	81%	$853

[2]Average amount paid is based on the total number of fraud complaints where amount paid was reported by West Virginia consumers (2,137).

IDENTITY THEFT Data Clearinghouse

Identity Theft Complaints from West Virginia Victims = 729

Identity Theft Types Reported by West Virginia Victims

Rank	Identity Theft Type	Complaints	Percentage[1]
1	Phone or Utilities Fraud	184	25%
2	Credit Card Fraud	178	24%
3	Bank Fraud[2]	102	14%
4	Government Documents or Benefits Fraud	57	8%
5	Employment-Related Fraud	42	6%
6	Loan Fraud	25	3%
	Other	198	27%
	Attempted Identity Theft	29	4%

[1]Percentages are based on the 729 victims reporting from West Virginia. Percentages add to more than 100 because approximately 15% of victims from West Virginia reported experiencing more than one type of identity theft.
[2]Includes fraud involving checking and savings accounts and electronic fund transfers.

WISCONSIN

Consumer Sentinel Complaint Figures
January 1 - December 31, 2007

Total Number of Fraud and Identity Theft Consumer Complaints = 12,302

ConsumerSentinel

Fraud Complaints from Wisconsin Consumers = 9,852

Top Fraud Complaint Categories for Wisconsin Consumers

Rank	Top Categories	Complaints	Percentage[1]
1	Shop-at-Home/Catalog Sales	1,078	11%
2	Internet Services	728	7%
3	Computer Equipment and Software	580	6%
4	Foreign Money Offers	537	5%
5	Prizes/Sweepstakes and Lotteries	410	4%

[1]Percentages are based on the total number of fraud complaints from Wisconsin consumers (9,852).

Amount Paid Reported by Wisconsin Consumers

Total No. of Complaints	Total Amount Paid Reported	Total Complaints Reporting Amt Pd	Percentage of Complaints Reporting Amount Paid	Average Amount Paid[2]
9,852	$12,735,185	9,007	91%	$1,414

[2]Average amount paid is based on the total number of fraud complaints where amount paid was reported by Wisconsin consumers (9,007). Three consumers reported an amount paid of $1 million or more.

IDENTITY THEFT Data Clearinghouse

Identity Theft Complaints from Wisconsin Victims = 2,450

Identity Theft Types Reported by Wisconsin Victims

Rank	Identity Theft Type	Complaints	Percentage[1]
1	Credit Card Fraud	635	26%
2	Phone or Utilities Fraud	387	16%
3	Bank Fraud[2]	373	15%
4	Employment-Related Fraud	286	12%
5	Government Documents or Benefits Fraud	239	10%
6	Loan Fraud	121	5%
	Other	617	25%
	Attempted Identity Theft	145	6%

[1]Percentages are based on the 2,450 victims reporting from Wisconsin. Percentages add to more than 100 because approximately 17% of victims from Wisconsin reported experiencing more than one type of identity theft.
[2]Includes fraud involving checking and savings accounts and electronic fund transfers.

WYOMING

Consumer Sentinel Complaint Figures
January 1 - December 31, 2007

Total Number of Fraud and Identity Theft Consumer Complaints = 1,106

ConsumerSentinel

Fraud Complaints from Wyoming Consumers = 884

Top Fraud Complaint Categories for Wyoming Consumers

Rank	Top Categories	Complaints	Percentage[1]
1	Shop-at-Home/Catalog Sales	109	12%
2	Internet Services	62	7%
3	Prizes/Sweepstakes and Lotteries	54	6%
4	Foreign Money Offers	54	6%
5	Internet Auctions	44	5%

[1]Percentages are based on the total number of fraud complaints from Wyoming consumers (884).

Amount Paid Reported by Wyoming Consumers

Total No. of Complaints	Total Amount Paid Reported	Total Complaints Reporting Amt Pd	Percentage of Complaints Reporting Amount Paid	Average Amount Paid[2]
884	$1,326,015	796	90%	$1,666

[2]Average amount paid is based on the total number of fraud complaints where amount paid was reported by Wyoming consumers (796).

IDENTITY THEFT Data Clearinghouse

Identity Theft Complaints from Wyoming Victims = 222

Identity Theft Types Reported by Wyoming Victims

Rank	Identity Theft Type	Complaints	Percentage[1]
1	Credit Card Fraud	47	21%
2	Employment-Related Fraud	33	15%
3	Phone or Utilities Fraud	30	14%
4	Bank Fraud[2]	26	12%
5	Government Documents or Benefits Fraud	14	6%
6	Loan Fraud	5	2%
	Other	71	32%
	Attempted Identity Theft	18	8%

[1]Percentages are based on the 222 victims reporting from Wyoming. Percentages add to more than 100 because approximately 12% of victims from Wyoming reported experiencing more than one type of identity theft.
[2]Includes fraud involving checking and savings accounts and electronic fund transfers.

Appendix A1: The Sentinel Network

The Identity Theft Data Clearinghouse was launched in November 1999 and is the sole national repository of consumer complaints about identity theft. The Clearinghouse provides specific investigative material for law enforcement and broader reports that provide insight to both private and public sector partners on ways to reduce the incidence of identity theft. Information in the Clearinghouse is available to law enforcement members via Consumer Sentinel, the secure, password-protected government Web site. This access enables law enforcers to readily spot identity theft problems in their own backyards, and to coordinate with other law enforcement officers where the data reveals common schemes or perpetrators.

Econsumer.gov was created in April 2001 to gather and share cross-border e-commerce complaints in order to respond to the challenges of multinational Internet fraud, and enhance consumer confidence in e-commerce. The multilingual public Web site provides general information about consumer protection in all countries that belong to the International Consumer Protection and Enforcement Network, contact information for consumer protection authorities in those countries, and an online complaint form. All information is available in English, French, German, Korean, Polish, and Spanish. Using the existing Consumer Sentinel Network, the incoming complaints are shared through the government Web site with participating consumer protection law enforcers from 23 nations.

Military Sentinel, which was established in September 2002, is a project of the Federal Trade Commission and the Department of Defense to identify and target consumer protection issues that affect members of the United States Armed Forces and their families. Military Sentinel also provides a gateway to consumer education materials covering a wide range of consumer protection issues, such as auto leasing, identity theft, and work-at-home scams. Members of the United States Armed Forces can enter complaints directly into Consumer Sentinel. Through Consumer Sentinel, the secure password-protected government Web site, this information is used by law enforcement agencies, members of the JAG staff, and others in the Department of Defense to help protect armed services members and their families from consumer protection-related problems.

IDENTITY THEFT
Data Clearinghouse

www.consumer.gov/idtheft

econsumer.gov

www.econsumer.gov

www.consumer.gov/military

APPENDIX A2: SENTINEL DATA CONTRIBUTORS[1] JANUARY 1 – DECEMBER 31, 2007

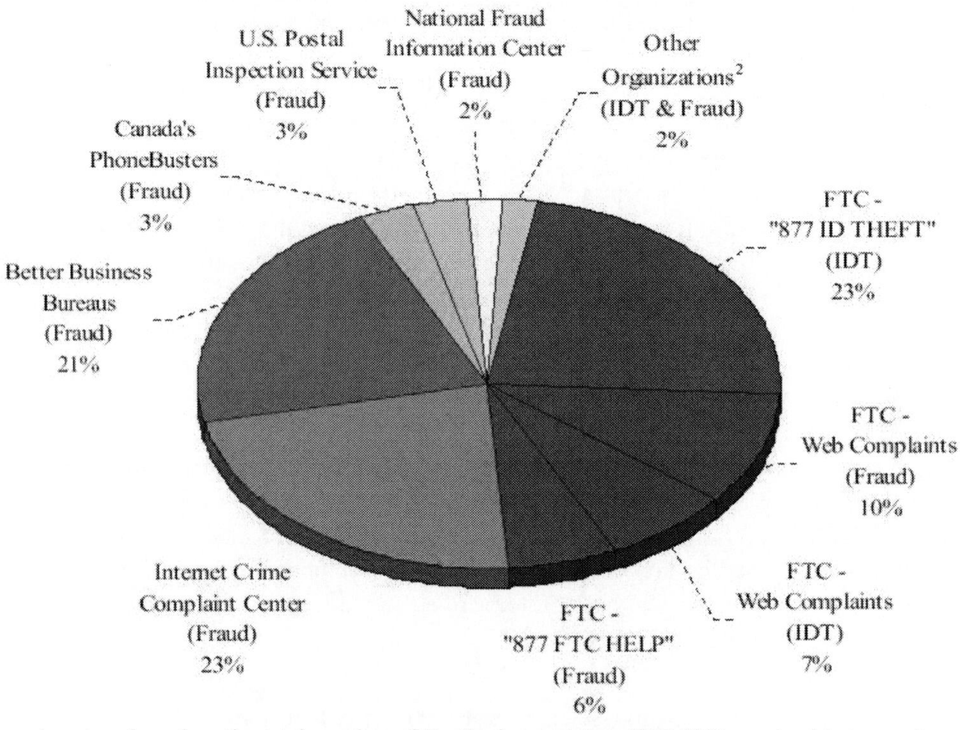

[1] Percentages are based on the total number of Sentinel complaints (**813,899**) received between January 1 and December 31, 2007. The type of complaints provided by the organization is indicated in parentheses.

[2] For a list of other organizations contributing to Sentinel, see Appendix A3.

APPENDIX A3: OTHER SENTINEL DATA CONTRIBUTORS JANUARY 1 – DECEMBER 31, 2007

Federal Agencies

Federal Bureau of Investigation
Office of the Comptroller of the Currency

Attorneys General Offices

Arkansas
District of Columbia
Nevada
North Dakota

Other State & Local Agencies

California, San Bernardino County District Attorney
California, Stanislaus County District Attorney
Georgia Governor's Office of Consumer Affairs
North Carolina Department of Justice
North Dakota Department of Financial Institutions
Wisconsin Department of Financial Institutions

Others

Identity Theft Assistance Center
Xerox Corporation

Local Police/Sheriff Departments

California, Inglewood Police Department
Colorado, Steamboat Springs Police Department
Connecticut, Danbury Police Department
Illinois, Broadview Police Department
Illinois, Chadwick Police Department
Illinois, Glenview Police Department
Illinois, Wilmette Police Department
Indiana, Fulton County Sheriff's Department
Iowa, Clinton Police Department
Kansas, Dodge City Police Department
Michigan, Genesee County Sheriff's Department
New Jersey, Harrison Township Police Department
New York, Cortland County Sheriff's Department
New York, DeWitt Police Department
New York, Suffern Police Department
North Carolina, Caldwell County Sheriff's office
Ohio, Streetsboro Police Department
Pennsylvania, Colonial Regional Police Department
Pennsylvania, Palmerton Police Department
Pennsylvania, Penn Township Police Department
Pennsylvania, Plymouth Township Police Department
Pennsylvania, Solebury Township Police Department
South Dakota, Miner County Sheriff's Office
Texas, Mansfield Police Department
Washington, Whatcom County Sheriff's Office

APPENDIX B: SENTINEL COMPLAINT CATEGORIES

Advance-Fee Loans and Credit Protection/Repair Offers: The promise of a loan that requires you to pay a fee first; worthless credit card loss protection and insurance programs; the promise that accurate negative information can be removed from your credit file for a fee; etc.
Business Opportunities and Work-at-Home Plans: Medical billing scams; misleading franchise and Internet-based business opportunities; wealth building plans that don't make good on their promises; etc.
Charitable Solicitations: Misleading pitches for donations to benefit local service organizations, solicitations for bogus charity or relief organization; etc.
Computer Equipment and Software: Problems with computer software, hardware, and computer equipment purchases; unwanted or unauthorized software installations and downloads; etc.
Debt Management/Credit Counseling: Unfulfilled promises by credit counseling organizations to provide free services, send payments to creditors in a timely manner, or reduce interest rates on credit card debt, eliminate late and over-the-limit fees; etc.
Employ Agencies/Job Counsel/Overseas Work: Unfulfilled, misleading and deceptive job placement opportunities; offers and services by employment-service firms for up-front fees; etc.
Foreign Money Offers: Letters or e-mails offering the "opportunity" to share in a percentage of millions of dollars that a self-proclaimed government official is trying to transfer illegally out of a foreign country in return for money, bank account numbers, or other identifying information from the victim.
Health Care: Fraudulent, misleading, or deceptive claims for vision correction procedures, dietary supplements, weight loss products or services, impotency treatments, health spas and equipment, infertility services, sunscreens, HIV test kits, etc.
Identity Theft: When someone appropriates your personal identifying information (like your Social Security number or credit card account number) to commit fraud or theft.
Internet Auctions: Non-delivery of goods; delivery of goods that are less valuable than advertised; lack of delivery in a timely way; failure to disclose all the relevant information about the product or terms of the sale; etc.
Internet Services: Trial offers from Internet Service Providers ("ISPs"); difficulty canceling an ISP account; issues with Internet entertainment services; undisclosed charges; website design and hosting services; spyware, adware, and malware issues; etc.
Investments: Promises of riches that don't pan out in day trading, oil and gas leases, gold and gems, FCC licenses, etc.
Magazines and Buyers Clubs: Pitches for "free," "pre-paid," or "special" magazine subscription deals and offers for club memberships that claim to help you save money when buying a particular product or service (CDs, books, etc.).
Multi-Level Marketing/Pyramids/Chain Letters: Network plans that offer commissions on the sale of goods by you and distributors you recruit.
Office Supplies and Services: Fraudulent or deceptive offers for toner, copier paper, maintenance supplies, equipment maintenance contracts; classified advertising and yellow page invoice scams; website cramming schemes; etc.
Prizes/Sweepstakes and Lotteries: Promotions for "free" prizes for a fee; foreign lotteries and sweepstakes offered through the phone, fax, e-mail or mail; etc.
Real Estate (Not Timeshares): Complaints about deceptive and misleading practices involving real estate-agents and companies, real estate appraisers and appraisal services, real estate-consultants, real estate-property management, and real estate land developers.
Shop-At-Home/Catalog Sales: Problems, such as undisclosed costs, failure to deliver on time, non-delivery, and refusal to honor a guarantee, with purchases made via the Internet (not including auction sales), telephone, or mail.
Telephone Services: Charges for calls to "toll-free" numbers; unauthorized charges such as charges for calls consumers didn't make; unauthorized switching of consumers' phone service provider; misleading pre-paid phone card offers; etc.
Travel, Vacations and Timeshare Plans: Deceptive offers for "free" or low-cost vacations; cut-rate student travel packages; misleading timeshare offers; etc.
"Other" complaint categories are: non-educational grants; unauthorized debits and charges for unknown products; DVD Video/film; modeling agencies/services; video games; scholarship/educational grants; dating services; property/inheritance tracers; green card application services; water purifiers; living trusts; and viaticals.

APPENDIX C1: FRAUD CONSUMER COMPLAINTS BY LARGEST METROPOLITAN AREAS (IN ALPHABETICAL ORDER)[1] JANUARY 1 – DECEMBER 31, 2007

Metropolitan Area	Complaints	Complaints Per 100,000 Population	Rank
Abilene, TX Metropolitan Statistical Area	237	149.9	360
Adrian, MI Micropolitan Statistical Area	298	291.6	75
Akron, OH Metropolitan Statistical Area	1,621	231.3	188
Albany, GA Metropolitan Statistical Area	303	184.8	297
Albany-Lebanon, OR Micropolitan Statistical Area	642	575.8	1
Albany-Schenectady-Troy, NY Metropolitan Statistical Area	1,710	201.0	261
Albuquerque, NM Metropolitan Statistical Area	1,525	186.7	292
Alexandria, LA Metropolitan Statistical Area	342	227.9	197
Allegan, MI Micropolitan Statistical Area	522	459.9	5
Allentown-Bethlehem-Easton, PA-NJ Metropolitan Statistical Area	1,850	231.2	189
Altoona, PA Metropolitan Statistical Area	234	185.0	296
Amarillo, TX Metropolitan Statistical Area	385	159.4	342
Anchorage, AK Metropolitan Statistical Area	942	262.3	116
Anderson, IN Metropolitan Statistical Area	403	308.6	61
Anderson, SC Metropolitan Statistical Area	404	227.0	200
Ann Arbor, MI Metropolitan Statistical Area	1,230	357.5	35
Anniston-Oxford, AL Metropolitan Statistical Area	226	200.2	264
Appleton, WI Metropolitan Statistical Area	707	325.3	50
Asheville, NC Metropolitan Statistical Area	900	226.1	204
Ashtabula, OH Micropolitan Statistical Area	269	261.9	118
Athens-Clarke County, GA Metropolitan Statistical Area	463	249.6	141
Atlanta-Sandy Springs-Marietta, GA Metropolitan Statistical Area	11,206	218.1	217
Atlantic City, NJ Metropolitan Statistical Area	748	275.4	95
Auburn-Opelika, AL Metropolitan Statistical Area	334	265.5	111
Augusta-Richmond County, GA-SC Metropolitan Statistical Area	891	170.3	328
Augusta-Waterville, ME Micropolitan Statistical Area	315	260.2	121
Austin-Round Rock, TX Metropolitan Statistical Area	4,164	275.1	96
Bakersfield, CA Metropolitan Statistical Area	1,412	181.0	305
Baltimore-Towson, MD Metropolitan Statistical Area	6,338	238.4	167
Bangor, ME Metropolitan Statistical Area	303	205.9	249
Barnstable Town, MA Metropolitan Statistical Area	384	170.8	326
Baton Rouge, LA Metropolitan Statistical Area	1,140	148.7	364
Battle Creek, MI Metropolitan Statistical Area	301	218.1	216

(Continued)

Metropolitan Area	Complaints	Complaints Per 100,000 Population	Rank
Bay City, MI Metropolitan Statistical Area	297	274.0	97
Beaumont-Port Arthur, TX Metropolitan Statistical Area	516	135.9	372
Bellingham, WA Metropolitan Statistical Area	628	337.7	45
Bend, OR Metropolitan Statistical Area	424	284.3	88
Billings, MT Metropolitan Statistical Area	310	209.3	240
Binghamton, NY Metropolitan Statistical Area	617	249.2	142
Birmingham-Hoover, AL Metropolitan Statistical Area	2,223	202.1	257
Bismarck, ND Metropolitan Statistical Area	117	115.7	378
Blacksburg-Christiansburg-Radford, VA Metropolitan Statistical Area	470	310.2	59
Bloomington, IN Metropolitan Statistical Area	529	296.0	72
Bloomington-Normal, IL Metropolitan Statistical Area	354	219.6	215
Bluefield, WV-VA Micropolitan Statistical Area	193	182.3	302
Boise City-Nampa, ID Metropolitan Statistical Area	1,285	226.4	202
Boston-Cambridge-Quincy, MA-NH Metropolitan Statistical Area	8,585	192.7	278
Boulder, CO Metropolitan Statistical Area	1,197	424.0	12
Bowling Green, KY Metropolitan Statistical Area	284	250.6	137
Bremerton-Silverdale, WA Metropolitan Statistical Area	653	271.4	101
Bridgeport-Stamford-Norwalk, CT Metropolitan Statistical Area	1,696	188.4	288
Brownsville-Harlingen, TX Metropolitan Statistical Area	224	57.8	382
Brunswick, GA Metropolitan Statistical Area	213	211.7	233
Buffalo-Niagara Falls, NY Metropolitan Statistical Area	1,709	150.2	357
Burlington, NC Metropolitan Statistical Area	355	248.8	144
Burlington-South Burlington, VT Metropolitan Statistical Area	333	161.6	337
Canton-Massillon, OH Metropolitan Statistical Area	740	180.6	306
Cape Coral-Fort Myers, FL Metropolitan Statistical Area	1,353	236.8	171
Cedar Rapids, IA Metropolitan Statistical Area	489	196.1	271
Chambersburg, PA Micropolitan Statistical Area	485	346.5	40
Champaign-Urbana, IL Metropolitan Statistical Area	393	181.5	304
Charleston, WV Metropolitan Statistical Area	459	150.2	358
Charleston-North Charleston, SC Metropolitan Statistical Area	1,078	178.7	311
Charlotte-Gastonia-Concord, NC-SC Metropolitan Statistical Area	4,214	266.2	107
Charlottesville, VA Metropolitan Statistical Area	493	259.1	122
Chattanooga, TN-GA Metropolitan Statistical Area	1,108	223.1	208
Chicago-Naperville-Joliet, IL-IN-WI Metropolitan Statistical Area	17,674	185.9	294
Chico, CA Metropolitan Statistical Area	536	248.3	145
Cincinnati-Middletown, OH-KY-IN Metropolitan Statistical Area	3,770	179.2	310
Clarksville, TN-KY Metropolitan Statistical Area	680	282.7	89
Cleveland, TN Metropolitan Statistical Area	314	286.8	82

(Continued)

Metropolitan Area	Complaints	Complaints Per 100,000 Population	Rank
Cleveland-Elyria-Mentor, OH Metropolitan Statistical Area	3,868	183.0	301
Coeur d'Alene, ID Metropolitan Statistical Area	430	327.0	48
College Station-Bryan, TX Metropolitan Statistical Area	381	198.3	270
Colorado Springs, CO Metropolitan Statistical Area	2,166	361.5	31
Columbia, MO Metropolitan Statistical Area	383	245.5	150
Columbia, SC Metropolitan Statistical Area	1,202	170.8	327
Columbus, GA-AL Metropolitan Statistical Area	585	202.5	256
Columbus, OH Metropolitan Statistical Area	4,783	277.2	94
Concord, NH Micropolitan Statistical Area	642	433.5	9
Corpus Christi, TX Metropolitan Statistical Area	623	149.8	361
Dallas-Fort Worth-Arlington, TX Metropolitan Statistical Area	12,467	207.6	245
Dalton, GA Metropolitan Statistical Area	395	293.9	73
Danville, VA Metropolitan Statistical Area	279	260.5	120
Daphne-Fairhope, AL Micropolitan Statistical Area	487	287.9	81
Davenport-Moline-Rock Island, IA-IL Metropolitan Statistical Area	622	164.9	334
Dayton, OH Metropolitan Statistical Area	1,946	232.0	186
Decatur, AL Metropolitan Statistical Area	269	179.9	308
Decatur, IL Metropolitan Statistical Area	170	155.5	345
Deltona-Daytona Beach-Ormond Beach, FL Metropolitan Statistical Area	1,146	230.8	190
Denver-Aurora, CO Metropolitan Statistical Area	6,889	286.0	84
Des Moines-West Des Moines, IA Metropolitan Statistical Area	994	186.1	293
Detroit-Warren-Livonia, MI Metropolitan Statistical Area	6,810	152.4	353
Dothan, AL Metropolitan Statistical Area	378	273.4	99
Dover, DE Metropolitan Statistical Area	310	210.0	237
Duluth, MN-WI Metropolitan Statistical Area	470	171.4	324
Dunn, NC Micropolitan Statistical Area	472	444.1	7
Durham, NC Metropolitan Statistical Area	1,780	383.3	21
East Liverpool-Salem, OH Micropolitan Statistical Area	257	232.5	184
East Stroudsburg, PA Micropolitan Statistical Area	602	363.3	27
Eau Claire, WI Metropolitan Statistical Area	335	216.1	222
El Centro, CA Metropolitan Statistical Area	215	134.1	374
El Paso, TX Metropolitan Statistical Area	988	134.2	373
Elizabethtown, KY Metropolitan Statistical Area	349	314.8	57
Elkhart-Goshen, IN Metropolitan Statistical Area	542	273.6	98
Erie, PA Metropolitan Statistical Area	564	201.6	260
Eugene-Springfield, OR Metropolitan Statistical Area	949	280.9	90
Eureka-Arcata-Fortuna, CA Micropolitan Statistical Area	250	194.8	277

(Continued)

Metropolitan Area	Complaints	Complaints Per 100,000 Population	Rank
Evansville, IN-KY Metropolitan Statistical Area	714	203.8	254
Fargo, ND-MN Metropolitan Statistical Area	280	149.7	362
Farmington, NM Metropolitan Statistical Area	190	150.2	359
Fayetteville, NC Metropolitan Statistical Area	896	262.5	115
Fayetteville-Springdale-Rogers, AR-MO Metropolitan Statistical Area	849	201.7	258
Flagstaff, AZ Metropolitan Statistical Area	448	358.5	34
Flint, MI Metropolitan Statistical Area	919	207.9	244
Florence, SC Metropolitan Statistical Area	311	156.4	344
Florence-Muscle Shoals, AL Metropolitan Statistical Area	238	166.8	330
Fort Collins-Loveland, CO Metropolitan Statistical Area	976	353.3	38
Fort Smith, AR-OK Metropolitan Statistical Area	463	160.3	339
Fort Walton Beach-Crestview-Destin, FL Metropolitan Statistical Area	622	345.0	41
Fort Wayne, IN Metropolitan Statistical Area	1,198	293.6	74
Fresno, CA Metropolitan Statistical Area	1,642	184.1	300
Gadsden, AL Metropolitan Statistical Area	202	195.4	273
Gainesville, FL Metropolitan Statistical Area	793	325.0	51
Gainesville, GA Metropolitan Statistical Area	740	427.1	10
Gettysburg, PA Micropolitan Statistical Area	415	410.5	15
Glens Falls, NY Metropolitan Statistical Area	261	201.6	259
Goldsboro, NC Metropolitan Statistical Area	235	206.4	247
Grand Junction, CO Metropolitan Statistical Area	383	285.4	85
Grand Rapids-Wyoming, MI Metropolitan Statistical Area	1,685	217.7	220
Greeley, CO Metropolitan Statistical Area	1,359	573.8	2
Green Bay, WI Metropolitan Statistical Area	615	205.7	250
Greensboro-High Point, NC Metropolitan Statistical Area	1,464	213.6	229
Greenville, NC Metropolitan Statistical Area	397	239.5	163
Greenville, SC Metropolitan Statistical Area	1,245	206.8	246
Gulfport-Biloxi, MS Metropolitan Statistical Area	550	241.3	158
Hagerstown-Martinsburg, MD-WV Metropolitan Statistical Area	770	298.9	69
Hammond, LA Micropolitan Statistical Area	340	300.5	67
Hanford-Corcoran, CA Metropolitan Statistical Area	519	355.1	36
Harrisburg-Carlisle, PA Metropolitan Statistical Area	1,300	247.4	148
Harrisonburg, VA Metropolitan Statistical Area	259	228.3	196
Hartford-West Hartford-East Hartford, CT Metropolitan Statistical Area	2,431	204.5	251
Hattiesburg, MS Metropolitan Statistical Area	249	184.8	298

(Continued)

Metropolitan Area	**Complaints**	**Complaints Per 100,000 Population**	**Rank**
Hickory-Lenoir-Morganton, NC Metropolitan Statistical Area	838	232.9	183
Hilo, HI Micropolitan Statistical Area	358	209.1	241
Hilton Head Island-Beaufort, SC Micropolitan Statistical Area	473	288.7	78
Holland-Grand Haven, MI Metropolitan Statistical Area	680	263.9	113
Homosassa Springs, FL Micropolitan Statistical Area	345	249.7	140
Honolulu, HI Metropolitan Statistical Area	1,827	200.8	263
Houma-Bayou Cane-Thibodaux, LA Metropolitan Statistical Area	235	115.8	377
Houston-Sugar Land-Baytown, TX Metropolitan Statistical Area	7,805	140.9	369
Huntington-Ashland, WV-KY-OH Metropolitan Statistical Area	499	174.8	319
Huntsville, AL Metropolitan Statistical Area	845	224.3	207
Idaho Falls, ID Metropolitan Statistical Area	275	235.1	178
Indianapolis-Carmel, IN Metropolitan Statistical Area	3,661	219.7	214
Iowa City, IA Metropolitan Statistical Area	397	284.5	87
Ithaca, NY Metropolitan Statistical Area	223	222.1	210
Jackson, MI Metropolitan Statistical Area	411	250.8	136
Jackson, MS Metropolitan Statistical Area	569	107.5	379
Jackson, TN Metropolitan Statistical Area	231	206.4	248
Jacksonville, FL Metropolitan Statistical Area	2,682	209.9	238
Jacksonville, NC Metropolitan Statistical Area	439	291.4	76
Jamestown-Dunkirk-Fredonia, NY Micropolitan Statistical Area	241	178.0	313
Janesville, WI Metropolitan Statistical Area	472	296.6	71
Jefferson City, MO Metropolitan Statistical Area	437	301.5	64
Johnson City, TN Metropolitan Statistical Area	597	312.3	58
Johnstown, PA Metropolitan Statistical Area	317	215.7	224
Jonesboro, AR Metropolitan Statistical Area	164	144.7	366
Joplin, MO Metropolitan Statistical Area	351	208.2	243
Kahului-Wailuku, HI Micropolitan Statistical Area	245	173.4	322
Kalamazoo-Portage, MI Metropolitan Statistical Area	890	278.4	93
Kankakee-Bradley, IL Metropolitan Statistical Area	258	236.5	173
Kansas City, MO-KS Metropolitan Statistical Area	3,951	200.8	262
Kennewick-Richland-Pasco, WA Metropolitan Statistical Area	534	236.2	174
Killeen-Temple-Fort Hood, TX Metropolitan Statistical Area	1,013	288.3	79
Kingsport-Bristol-Bristol, TN-VA Metropolitan Statistical Area	771	254.9	131
Kingston, NY Metropolitan Statistical Area	472	258.3	125
Knoxville, TN Metropolitan Statistical Area	1,726	258.6	124
Kokomo, IN Metropolitan Statistical Area	241	238.9	166
La Crosse, WI-MN Metropolitan Statistical Area	273	211.2	234
Lafayette, IN Metropolitan Statistical Area	473	254.7	132

(Continued)

Metropolitan Area	Complaints	Complaints Per 100,000 Population	Rank
Lafayette, LA Metropolitan Statistical Area	519	204.0	253
Lake Charles, LA Metropolitan Statistical Area	367	190.8	283
Lake Havasu City-Kingman, AZ Micropolitan Statistical Area	676	350.2	39
Lakeland, FL Metropolitan Statistical Area	1,350	240.4	160
Lancaster, PA Metropolitan Statistical Area	1,166	235.8	176
Lansing-East Lansing, MI Metropolitan Statistical Area	848	186.8	291
Laredo, TX Metropolitan Statistical Area	148	63.9	381
Las Cruces, NM Metropolitan Statistical Area	475	245.0	151
Las Vegas-Paradise, NV Metropolitan Statistical Area	3,555	200.0	265
Lawrence, KS Metropolitan Statistical Area	268	239.0	164
Lawton, OK Metropolitan Statistical Area	248	227.1	199
Lebanon, NH-VT Micropolitan Statistical Area	458	265.6	109
Lebanon, PA Metropolitan Statistical Area	449	353.9	37
Lewiston-Auburn, ME Metropolitan Statistical Area	301	279.9	92
Lexington-Fayette, KY Metropolitan Statistical Area	966	221.2	211
Lima, OH Metropolitan Statistical Area	226	213.6	228
Lincoln, NE Metropolitan Statistical Area	611	215.2	226
Little Rock-North Little Rock, AR Metropolitan Statistical Area	1,228	188.1	289
Logan, UT-ID Metropolitan Statistical Area	253	227.6	198
Longview, TX Metropolitan Statistical Area	509	250.3	138
Los Angeles-Long Beach-Santa Ana, CA Metropolitan Statistical Area	20,775	160.4	338
Louisville-Jefferson County, KY-IN Metropolitan Statistical Area	2,334	191.0	282
Lubbock, TX Metropolitan Statistical Area	469	179.4	309
Lumberton, NC Micropolitan Statistical Area	196	151.9	356
Lynchburg, VA Metropolitan Statistical Area	636	265.5	110
Macon, GA Metropolitan Statistical Area	724	315.7	55
Madera, CA Metropolitan Statistical Area	527	360.1	33
Madison, WI Metropolitan Statistical Area	1,359	250.3	139
Manchester-Nashua, NH Metropolitan Statistical Area	1,311	325.5	49
Manhattan, KS Micropolitan Statistical Area	247	233.2	182
Mansfield, OH Metropolitan Statistical Area	335	263.8	114
McAllen-Edinburg-Mission, TX Metropolitan Statistical Area	452	64.5	380
Medford, OR Metropolitan Statistical Area	591	299.9	68
Memphis, TN-MS-AR Metropolitan Statistical Area	1,827	143.3	367
Merced, CA Metropolitan Statistical Area	432	175.9	317
Meridian, MS Micropolitan Statistical Area	159	152.2	355
Miami-Fort Lauderdale-Miami Beach, FL Metropolitan Statistical Area	8,931	163.5	336
Michigan City-La Porte, IN Metropolitan Statistical Area	448	405.5	17

(Continued)

Metropolitan Area	Complaints	Complaints Per 100,000 Population	Rank
Midland, TX Metropolitan Statistical Area	207	166.4	332
Milwaukee-Waukesha-West Allis, WI Metropolitan Statistical Area	3,288	217.8	218
Minneapolis-St. Paul-Bloomington, MN-WI Metropolitan Statistical Area	7,156	225.4	206
Missoula, MT Metropolitan Statistical Area	321	316.5	54
Mobile, AL Metropolitan Statistical Area	634	156.9	343
Modesto, CA Metropolitan Statistical Area	1,087	212.2	232
Monroe, LA Metropolitan Statistical Area	264	153.3	351
Monroe, MI Metropolitan Statistical Area	652	420.6	13
Montgomery, AL Metropolitan Statistical Area	637	176.1	316
Morgantown, WV Metropolitan Statistical Area	343	297.9	70
Morristown, TN Metropolitan Statistical Area	319	240.1	162
Mount Vernon-Anacortes, WA Metropolitan Statistical Area	472	408.0	16
Muncie, IN Metropolitan Statistical Area	266	231.5	187
Muskegon-Norton Shores, MI Metropolitan Statistical Area	374	213.4	230
Myrtle Beach-Conway-North Myrtle Beach, SC Metropolitan Statistical Area	642	269.2	105
Napa, CA Metropolitan Statistical Area	703	526.5	3
Naples-Marco Island, FL Metropolitan Statistical Area	659	209.4	239
Nashville-Davidson--Murfreesboro, TN Metropolitan Statistical Area	3,601	247.5	147
New Bern, NC Micropolitan Statistical Area	458	388.6	19
New Haven-Milford, CT Metropolitan Statistical Area	1,823	215.7	225
New Orleans-Metairie-Kenner, LA Metropolitan Statistical Area	1,905	185.9	295
New York-Northern New Jersey-Long Island, NY-NJ-PA Metropolitan Statistical Area	29,207	155.2	347
Niles-Benton Harbor, MI Metropolitan Statistical Area	606	374.8	24
Norwich-New London, CT Metropolitan Statistical Area	714	271.2	102
Ocala, FL Metropolitan Statistical Area	772	244.2	154
Odessa, TX Metropolitan Statistical Area	181	142.0	368
Ogden-Clearfield, UT Metropolitan Statistical Area	1,271	255.4	130
Ogdensburg-Massena, NY Micropolitan Statistical Area	171	153.7	350
Oklahoma City, OK Metropolitan Statistical Area	2,090	178.3	312
Olympia, WA Metropolitan Statistical Area	895	381.4	22
Omaha-Council Bluffs, NE-IA Metropolitan Statistical Area	1,636	198.9	268
Orlando-Kissimmee, FL Metropolitan Statistical Area	4,418	222.6	209
Oshkosh-Neenah, WI Metropolitan Statistical Area	510	317.6	53
Ottawa-Streator, IL Micropolitan Statistical Area	336	217.7	219
Owensboro, KY Metropolitan Statistical Area	353	314.9	56

(Continued)

Metropolitan Area	**Complaints**	**Complaints Per 100,000 Population**	**Rank**
Oxnard-Thousand Oaks-Ventura, CA Metropolitan Statistical Area	1,950	243.8	155
Palm Bay-Melbourne-Titusville, FL Metropolitan Statistical Area	1,004	187.9	290
Panama City-Lynn Haven, FL Metropolitan Statistical Area	422	258.1	126
Parkersburg-Marietta-Vienna, WV-OH Metropolitan Statistical Area	258	159.5	341
Pascagoula, MS Metropolitan Statistical Area	444	291.3	77
Pensacola-Ferry Pass-Brent, FL Metropolitan Statistical Area	1,031	234.3	180
Peoria, IL Metropolitan Statistical Area	575	155.3	346
Philadelphia-Camden-Wilmington, PA-NJ-DE-MD Metropolitan Statistical Area	10,214	175.3	318
Phoenix-Mesa-Scottsdale, AZ Metropolitan Statistical Area	9,930	245.8	149
Pine Bluff, AR Metropolitan Statistical Area	181	174.6	320
Pittsburgh, PA Metropolitan Statistical Area	4,485	189.2	287
Pittsfield, MA Metropolitan Statistical Area	283	215.8	223
Port St. Lucie-Fort Pierce, FL Metropolitan Statistical Area	942	240.2	161
Portland-South Portland-Biddeford, ME Metropolitan Statistical Area	1,166	227.0	201
Portland-Vancouver-Beaverton, OR-WA Metropolitan Statistical Area	5,236	245.0	152
Pottsville, PA Micropolitan Statistical Area	486	329.7	46
Poughkeepsie-Newburgh-Middletown, NY Metropolitan Statistical Area	1,312	195.4	274
Prescott, AZ Metropolitan Statistical Area	859	413.0	14
Providence-New Bedford-Fall River, RI-MA Metropolitan Statistical Area	2,683	166.3	333
Provo-Orem, UT Metropolitan Statistical Area	1,433	302.2	63
Pueblo, CO Metropolitan Statistical Area	305	199.5	267
Punta Gorda, FL Metropolitan Statistical Area	790	511.5	4
Racine, WI Metropolitan Statistical Area	710	362.1	29
Raleigh-Cary, NC Metropolitan Statistical Area	2,692	270.7	103
Rapid City, SD Metropolitan Statistical Area	183	154.1	348
Reading, PA Metropolitan Statistical Area	966	240.8	159
Redding, CA Metropolitan Statistical Area	415	230.6	191
Reno-Sparks, NV Metropolitan Statistical Area	1,310	327.0	47
Richmond, VA Metropolitan Statistical Area	2,700	226.1	203
Riverside-San Bernardino-Ontario, CA Metropolitan Statistical Area	6,153	152.8	352
Roanoke, VA Metropolitan Statistical Area	895	303.3	62

(Continued)

Metropolitan Area	Complaints	Complaints Per 100,000 Population	Rank
Rochester, MN Metropolitan Statistical Area	414	230.5	192
Rochester, NY Metropolitan Statistical Area	1,527	147.5	365
Rockford, IL Metropolitan Statistical Area	712	204.4	252
Rocky Mount, NC Metropolitan Statistical Area	346	236.5	172
Roseburg, OR Micropolitan Statistical Area	481	457.6	6
Sacramento--Arden-Arcade--Roseville, CA Metropolitan Statistical Area	4,747	229.6	193
Saginaw-Saginaw Township North, MI Metropolitan Statistical Area	522	253.0	134
Salem, OR Metropolitan Statistical Area	1,102	286.5	83
Salinas, CA Metropolitan Statistical Area	781	190.4	284
Salisbury, MD Metropolitan Statistical Area	279	236.9	170
Salisbury, NC Micropolitan Statistical Area	523	383.8	20
Salt Lake City, UT Metropolitan Statistical Area	2,786	260.9	119
San Angelo, TX Metropolitan Statistical Area	174	164.5	335
San Antonio, TX Metropolitan Statistical Area	3,364	173.2	323
San Diego-Carlsbad-San Marcos, CA Metropolitan Statistical Area	7,123	242.2	156
San Francisco-Oakland-Fremont, CA Metropolitan Statistical Area	9,760	233.5	181
San Jose-Sunnyvale-Santa Clara, CA Metropolitan Statistical Area	4,577	256.1	127
San Luis Obispo-Paso Robles, CA Metropolitan Statistical Area	614	238.9	165
Santa Barbara-Santa Maria, CA Metropolitan Statistical Area	835	208.6	242
Santa Cruz-Watsonville, CA Metropolitan Statistical Area	1,011	404.9	18
Santa Fe, NM Metropolitan Statistical Area	353	247.9	146
Santa Rosa-Petaluma, CA Metropolitan Statistical Area	1,101	235.8	175
Sarasota-Bradenton-Venice, FL Metropolitan Statistical Area	1,542	225.8	205
Savannah, GA Metropolitan Statistical Area	692	216.2	221
Scranton--Wilkes-Barre, PA Metropolitan Statistical Area	1,000	181.5	303
Seaford, DE Micropolitan Statistical Area	387	214.7	227
Seattle-Tacoma-Bellevue, WA Metropolitan Statistical Area	8,697	266.5	106
Sebastian-Vero Beach, FL Metropolitan Statistical Area	324	249.0	143
Sheboygan, WI Metropolitan Statistical Area	253	220.5	212
Sherman-Denison, TX Metropolitan Statistical Area	313	264.2	112
Shreveport-Bossier City, LA Metropolitan Statistical Area	684	176.8	314
Sierra Vista-Douglas, AZ Micropolitan Statistical Area	461	360.8	32
Sioux City, IA-NE-SD Metropolitan Statistical Area	221	154.0	349
Sioux Falls, SD Metropolitan Statistical Area	355	166.7	331
South Bend-Mishawaka, IN-MI Metropolitan Statistical Area	957	300.9	65

(Continued)

Metropolitan Area	**Complaints**	**Complaints Per 100,000 Population**	**Rank**
Spartanburg, SC Metropolitan Statistical Area	629	232.0	185
Spokane, WA Metropolitan Statistical Area	1,448	324.2	52
Springfield, IL Metropolitan Statistical Area	314	152.3	354
Springfield, MA Metropolitan Statistical Area	1,340	195.3	275
Springfield, MO Metropolitan Statistical Area	970	238.3	168
Springfield, OH Metropolitan Statistical Area	513	361.6	30
St. Cloud, MN Metropolitan Statistical Area	479	262.1	117
St. George, UT Metropolitan Statistical Area	364	288.2	80
St. Joseph, MO-KS Metropolitan Statistical Area	248	202.8	255
St. Louis, MO-IL Metropolitan Statistical Area	8,641	309.0	60
State College, PA Metropolitan Statistical Area	270	191.6	280
Statesville-Mooresville, NC Micropolitan Statistical Area	544	372.1	25
Staunton-Waynesboro, VA Micropolitan Statistical Area	296	255.8	128
Stockton, CA Metropolitan Statistical Area	1,414	210.1	236
Sumter, SC Metropolitan Statistical Area	230	220.2	213
Syracuse, NY Metropolitan Statistical Area	1,113	171.2	325
Tallahassee, FL Metropolitan Statistical Area	657	195.2	276
Tampa-St. Petersburg-Clearwater, FL Metropolitan Statistical Area	6,896	255.6	129
Terre Haute, IN Metropolitan Statistical Area	386	229.5	194
Texarkana, TX-Texarkana, AR Metropolitan Statistical Area	234	174.0	321
Thomasville-Lexington, NC Micropolitan Statistical Area	667	426.9	11
Toledo, OH Metropolitan Statistical Area	1,250	191.2	281
Topeka, KS Metropolitan Statistical Area	618	270.0	104
Torrington, CT Micropolitan Statistical Area	698	367.1	26
Traverse City, MI Micropolitan Statistical Area	427	300.6	66
Trenton-Ewing, NJ Metropolitan Statistical Area	934	254.1	133
Tucson, AZ Metropolitan Statistical Area	2,448	258.7	123
Tulsa, OK Metropolitan Statistical Area	1,706	190.0	286
Tupelo, MS Micropolitan Statistical Area	251	190.2	285
Tuscaloosa, AL Metropolitan Statistical Area	366	184.1	299
Tyler, TX Metropolitan Statistical Area	457	234.8	179
Utica-Rome, NY Metropolitan Statistical Area	476	160.1	340
Valdosta, GA Metropolitan Statistical Area	266	210.6	235
Vallejo-Fairfield, CA Metropolitan Statistical Area	1,395	338.9	43
Victoria, TX Metropolitan Statistical Area	144	126.2	376
Vineland-Millville-Bridgeton, NJ Metropolitan Statistical Area	203	131.1	375
Virginia Beach-Norfolk-Newport News, VA-NC Metropolitan Statistical Area	3,295	199.8	266
Visalia-Porterville, CA Metropolitan Statistical Area	715	170.3	329

(Continued)

Metropolitan Area	Complaints	Complaints Per 100,000 Population	Rank
Waco, TX Metropolitan Statistical Area	408	180.4	307
Warner Robins, GA Metropolitan Statistical Area	363	284.6	86
Washington-Arlington-Alexandria, DC-VA-MD-WV Metropolitan Statistical Area	13,291	251.2	135
Waterloo-Cedar Falls, IA Metropolitan Statistical Area	242	149.1	363
Watertown-Fort Drum, NY Micropolitan Statistical Area	243	212.7	231
Wausau, WI Metropolitan Statistical Area	449	344.8	42
Weirton-Steubenville, WV-OH Metropolitan Statistical Area	340	271.6	100
Wenatchee, WA Metropolitan Statistical Area	284	265.9	108
Wheeling, WV-OH Metropolitan Statistical Area	207	140.5	370
Whitewater, WI Micropolitan Statistical Area	380	376.2	23
Wichita Falls, TX Metropolitan Statistical Area	289	198.6	269
Wichita, KS Metropolitan Statistical Area	830	140.2	371
Williamsport, PA Metropolitan Statistical Area	269	228.6	195
Willimantic, CT Micropolitan Statistical Area	518	443.2	8
Wilmington, NC Metropolitan Statistical Area	788	241.6	157
Winchester, VA-WV Metropolitan Statistical Area	402	338.0	44
Winston-Salem, NC Metropolitan Statistical Area	1,085	237.6	169
Wooster, OH Micropolitan Statistical Area	319	279.9	91
Worcester, MA Metropolitan Statistical Area	1,917	244.2	153
Yakima, WA Metropolitan Statistical Area	448	192.2	279
York-Hanover, PA Metropolitan Statistical Area	979	235.2	177
Youngstown-Warren-Boardman, OH-PA Metropolitan Statistical Area	1,151	196.1	272
Yuba City, CA Metropolitan Statistical Area	586	362.2	28
Yuma, AZ Metropolitan Statistical Area	331	176.5	315

[1] Ranking is based on the number of fraud complaints per 100,000 inhabitants for each Metropolitan Area. This chart illustrates Metropolitan Areas (Metropolitan and Micropolitan Statistical Areas) with a population of one hundred thousand or more. Metropolitan Areas presented here are those defined by the Office of Management and Budget as of December 2005 and the population estimates are based on the 2006 U.S. Census table CBSA-EST2006-01.

Appendix C2: Identity Theft Consumer Complaints by Largest Metropolitan Areas (in alphabetical order)[1] January 1 – December 31, 2007

Metropolitan Area	Complaints	Complaints Per 100,000 Population	Rank
Abilene, TX Metropolitan Statistical Area	120	75.9	271
Adrian, MI Micropolitan Statistical Area	96	93.9	166
Akron, OH Metropolitan Statistical Area	733	104.6	120
Albany, GA Metropolitan Statistical Area	216	131.7	61
Albany-Lebanon, OR Micropolitan Statistical Area	183	164.1	19
Albany-Schenectady-Troy, NY Metropolitan Statistical Area	640	75.2	276
Albuquerque, NM Metropolitan Statistical Area	1,049	128.4	66
Alexandria, LA Metropolitan Statistical Area	134	89.3	198
Allegan, MI Micropolitan Statistical Area	123	108.4	107
Allentown-Bethlehem-Easton, PA-NJ Metropolitan Statistical Area	844	105.5	116
Altoona, PA Metropolitan Statistical Area	102	80.6	242
Amarillo, TX Metropolitan Statistical Area	291	120.5	80
Anchorage, AK Metropolitan Statistical Area	190	52.9	352
Anderson, IN Metropolitan Statistical Area	126	96.5	152
Anderson, SC Metropolitan Statistical Area	207	116.3	87
Ann Arbor, MI Metropolitan Statistical Area	487	141.6	44
Anniston-Oxford, AL Metropolitan Statistical Area	115	101.9	130
Appleton, WI Metropolitan Statistical Area	132	60.7	332
Asheville, NC Metropolitan Statistical Area	303	76.1	268
Ashtabula, OH Micropolitan Statistical Area	67	65.2	318
Athens-Clarke County, GA Metropolitan Statistical Area	191	103.0	128
Atlanta-Sandy Springs-Marietta, GA Metropolitan Statistical Area	6,223	121.1	79
Atlantic City, NJ Metropolitan Statistical Area	310	114.1	95
Auburn-Opelika, AL Metropolitan Statistical Area	148	117.7	86
Augusta-Richmond County, GA-SC Metropolitan Statistical Area	445	85.0	221
Augusta-Waterville, ME Micropolitan Statistical Area	65	53.7	349
Austin-Round Rock, TX Metropolitan Statistical Area	1,641	108.4	106
Bakersfield, CA Metropolitan Statistical Area	1,436	184.1	14
Baltimore-Towson, MD Metropolitan Statistical Area	2,631	99.0	146
Bangor, ME Metropolitan Statistical Area	83	56.4	342
Barnstable Town, MA Metropolitan Statistical Area	154	68.5	301
Baton Rouge, LA Metropolitan Statistical Area	632	82.5	236

Table. (Continued)

Metropolitan Area	Complaints	Complaints Per 100,000 Population	Rank
Battle Creek, MI Metropolitan Statistical Area	91	65.9	313
Bay City, MI Metropolitan Statistical Area	103	95.0	160
Beaumont-Port Arthur, TX Metropolitan Statistical Area	303	79.8	247
Bellingham, WA Metropolitan Statistical Area	172	92.5	174
Bend, OR Metropolitan Statistical Area	102	68.4	302
Billings, MT Metropolitan Statistical Area	76	51.3	355
Binghamton, NY Metropolitan Statistical Area	160	64.6	322
Birmingham-Hoover, AL Metropolitan Statistical Area	1,054	95.8	156
Bismarck, ND Metropolitan Statistical Area	34	33.6	380
Blacksburg-Christiansburg-Radford, VA Metropolitan Statistical Area	81	53.5	350
Bloomington, IN Metropolitan Statistical Area	142	79.5	251
Bloomington-Normal, IL Metropolitan Statistical Area	117	72.6	288
Bluefield, WV-VA Micropolitan Statistical Area	59	55.7	344
Boise City-Nampa, ID Metropolitan Statistical Area	378	66.6	309
Boston-Cambridge-Quincy, MA-NH Metropolitan Statistical Area	3,302	74.1	281
Boulder, CO Metropolitan Statistical Area	327	115.8	89
Bowling Green, KY Metropolitan Statistical Area	99	87.4	214
Bremerton-Silverdale, WA Metropolitan Statistical Area	181	75.2	275
Bridgeport-Stamford-Norwalk, CT Metropolitan Statistical Area	829	92.1	176
Brownsville-Harlingen, TX Metropolitan Statistical Area	876	225.9	4
Brunswick, GA Metropolitan Statistical Area	77	76.5	265
Buffalo-Niagara Falls, NY Metropolitan Statistical Area	732	64.4	324
Burlington, NC Metropolitan Statistical Area	144	100.9	132
Burlington-South Burlington, VT Metropolitan Statistical Area	89	43.2	371
Canton-Massillon, OH Metropolitan Statistical Area	254	62.0	329
Cape Coral-Fort Myers, FL Metropolitan Statistical Area	573	100.3	136
Cedar Rapids, IA Metropolitan Statistical Area	101	40.5	374
Chambersburg, PA Micropolitan Statistical Area	147	105.0	119
Champaign-Urbana, IL Metropolitan Statistical Area	98	45.2	366
Charleston, WV Metropolitan Statistical Area	150	49.1	360
Charleston-North Charleston, SC Metropolitan Statistical Area	441	73.1	283
Charlotte-Gastonia-Concord, NC-SC Metropolitan Statistical Area	1,664	105.1	118
Charlottesville, VA Metropolitan Statistical Area	174	91.4	181
Chattanooga, TN-GA Metropolitan Statistical Area	465	93.6	168
Chicago-Naperville-Joliet, IL-IN-WI Metropolitan Statistical Area	9,082	95.5	158
Chico, CA Metropolitan Statistical Area	216	100.1	138

(Continued)

Metropolitan Area	**Complaints**	**Complaints Per 100,000 Population**	**Rank**
Cincinnati-Middletown, OH-KY-IN Metropolitan Statistical Area	1,358	64.5	323
Clarksville, TN-KY Metropolitan Statistical Area	201	83.6	229
Cleveland, TN Metropolitan Statistical Area	149	136.1	51
Cleveland-Elyria-Mentor, OH Metropolitan Statistical Area	1,926	91.1	185
Coeur d'Alene, ID Metropolitan Statistical Area	102	77.6	262
College Station-Bryan, TX Metropolitan Statistical Area	176	91.6	179
Colorado Springs, CO Metropolitan Statistical Area	545	91.0	188
Columbia, MO Metropolitan Statistical Area	112	71.8	291
Columbia, SC Metropolitan Statistical Area	570	81.0	240
Columbus, GA-AL Metropolitan Statistical Area	320	110.8	103
Columbus, OH Metropolitan Statistical Area	1,402	81.2	239
Concord, NH Micropolitan Statistical Area	137	92.5	173
Corpus Christi, TX Metropolitan Statistical Area	558	134.2	56
Dallas-Fort Worth-Arlington, TX Metropolitan Statistical Area	7,978	132.9	59
Dalton, GA Metropolitan Statistical Area	172	128.0	68
Danville, VA Metropolitan Statistical Area	105	98.1	149
Daphne-Fairhope, AL Micropolitan Statistical Area	181	107.0	111
Davenport-Moline-Rock Island, IA-IL Metropolitan Statistical Area	177	46.9	364
Dayton, OH Metropolitan Statistical Area	603	71.9	290
Decatur, AL Metropolitan Statistical Area	141	94.3	163
Decatur, IL Metropolitan Statistical Area	83	75.9	270
Deltona-Daytona Beach-Ormond Beach, FL Metropolitan Statistical Area	465	93.6	167
Denver-Aurora, CO Metropolitan Statistical Area	2,730	113.3	97
Des Moines-West Des Moines, IA Metropolitan Statistical Area	233	43.6	370
Detroit-Warren-Livonia, MI Metropolitan Statistical Area	4,632	103.6	125
Dothan, AL Metropolitan Statistical Area	190	137.4	49
Dover, DE Metropolitan Statistical Area	134	90.8	191
Duluth, MN-WI Metropolitan Statistical Area	136	49.6	359
Dunn, NC Micropolitan Statistical Area	223	209.8	8
Durham, NC Metropolitan Statistical Area	675	145.4	38
East Liverpool-Salem, OH Micropolitan Statistical Area	120	108.6	105
East Stroudsburg, PA Micropolitan Statistical Area	225	135.8	54
Eau Claire, WI Metropolitan Statistical Area	34	21.9	382
El Centro, CA Metropolitan Statistical Area	230	143.5	40
El Paso, TX Metropolitan Statistical Area	908	123.3	74
Elizabethtown, KY Metropolitan Statistical Area	93	83.9	224

(Continued)

Metropolitan Area	Complaints	Complaints Per 100,000 Population	Rank
Elkhart-Goshen, IN Metropolitan Statistical Area	212	107.0	110
Erie, PA Metropolitan Statistical Area	185	66.1	311
Eugene-Springfield, OR Metropolitan Statistical Area	236	69.8	296
Eureka-Arcata-Fortuna, CA Micropolitan Statistical Area	94	73.2	282
Evansville, IN-KY Metropolitan Statistical Area	197	56.2	343
Fargo, ND-MN Metropolitan Statistical Area	83	44.4	368
Farmington, NM Metropolitan Statistical Area	100	79.1	256
Fayetteville, NC Metropolitan Statistical Area	423	123.9	72
Fayetteville-Springdale-Rogers, AR-MO Metropolitan Statistical Area	285	67.7	303
Flagstaff, AZ Metropolitan Statistical Area	261	208.9	9
Flint, MI Metropolitan Statistical Area	366	82.8	232
Florence, SC Metropolitan Statistical Area	176	88.5	206
Florence-Muscle Shoals, AL Metropolitan Statistical Area	93	65.2	319
Fort Collins-Loveland, CO Metropolitan Statistical Area	262	94.8	161
Fort Smith, AR-OK Metropolitan Statistical Area	188	65.1	320
Fort Walton Beach-Crestview-Destin, FL Metropolitan Statistical Area	205	113.7	96
Fort Wayne, IN Metropolitan Statistical Area	342	83.8	226
Fresno, CA Metropolitan Statistical Area	1,358	152.3	30
Gadsden, AL Metropolitan Statistical Area	134	129.6	64
Gainesville, FL Metropolitan Statistical Area	206	84.4	222
Gainesville, GA Metropolitan Statistical Area	307	177.2	16
Gettysburg, PA Micropolitan Statistical Area	123	121.7	78
Glens Falls, NY Metropolitan Statistical Area	98	75.7	272
Goldsboro, NC Metropolitan Statistical Area	146	128.2	67
Grand Junction, CO Metropolitan Statistical Area	129	96.1	154
Grand Rapids-Wyoming, MI Metropolitan Statistical Area	516	66.7	308
Greeley, CO Metropolitan Statistical Area	540	228.0	3
Green Bay, WI Metropolitan Statistical Area	116	38.8	377
Greensboro-High Point, NC Metropolitan Statistical Area	615	89.7	196
Greenville, NC Metropolitan Statistical Area	222	133.9	58
Greenville, SC Metropolitan Statistical Area	554	92.0	177
Gulfport-Biloxi, MS Metropolitan Statistical Area	225	98.7	148
Hagerstown-Martinsburg, MD-WV Metropolitan Statistical Area	205	79.6	249
Hammond, LA Micropolitan Statistical Area	169	149.4	35
Hanford-Corcoran, CA Metropolitan Statistical Area	314	214.8	7
Harrisburg-Carlisle, PA Metropolitan Statistical Area	383	72.9	285
Harrisonburg, VA Metropolitan Statistical Area	95	83.7	227

(Continued)

Metropolitan Area	Complaints	Complaints Per 100,000 Population	Rank
Hartford-West Hartford-East Hartford, CT Metropolitan Statistical Area	1,028	86.5	216
Hattiesburg, MS Metropolitan Statistical Area	105	77.9	259
Hickory-Lenoir-Morganton, NC Metropolitan Statistical Area	347	96.4	153
Hilo, HI Micropolitan Statistical Area	55	32.1	381
Hilton Head Island-Beaufort, SC Micropolitan Statistical Area	203	123.9	73
Holland-Grand Haven, MI Metropolitan Statistical Area	179	69.5	300
Homosassa Springs, FL Micropolitan Statistical Area	130	94.1	165
Honolulu, HI Metropolitan Statistical Area	499	54.8	346
Houma-Bayou Cane-Thibodaux, LA Metropolitan Statistical Area	120	59.1	338
Houston-Sugar Land-Baytown, TX Metropolitan Statistical Area	6,443	116.3	88
Huntington-Ashland, WV-KY-OH Metropolitan Statistical Area	161	56.4	341
Huntsville, AL Metropolitan Statistical Area	240	63.7	325
Idaho Falls, ID Metropolitan Statistical Area	85	72.7	287
Indianapolis-Carmel, IN Metropolitan Statistical Area	1,541	92.5	175
Iowa City, IA Metropolitan Statistical Area	105	75.2	274
Ithaca, NY Metropolitan Statistical Area	48	47.8	363
Jackson, MI Metropolitan Statistical Area	108	65.9	314
Jackson, MS Metropolitan Statistical Area	494	93.3	171
Jackson, TN Metropolitan Statistical Area	97	86.7	215
Jacksonville, FL Metropolitan Statistical Area	1,330	104.1	124
Jacksonville, NC Metropolitan Statistical Area	150	99.6	141
Jamestown-Dunkirk-Fredonia, NY Micropolitan Statistical Area	75	55.4	345
Janesville, WI Metropolitan Statistical Area	141	88.6	204
Jefferson City, MO Metropolitan Statistical Area	151	104.2	123
Johnson City, TN Metropolitan Statistical Area	174	91.0	187
Johnstown, PA Metropolitan Statistical Area	140	95.3	159
Jonesboro, AR Metropolitan Statistical Area	82	72.4	289
Joplin, MO Metropolitan Statistical Area	142	84.2	223
Kahului-Wailuku, HI Micropolitan Statistical Area	52	36.8	379
Kalamazoo-Portage, MI Metropolitan Statistical Area	284	88.8	201
Kankakee-Bradley, IL Metropolitan Statistical Area	118	108.2	108
Kansas City, MO-KS Metropolitan Statistical Area	1,539	78.2	258
Kennewick-Richland-Pasco, WA Metropolitan Statistical Area	211	93.3	170
Killeen-Temple-Fort Hood, TX Metropolitan Statistical Area	404	115.0	91
Kingsport-Bristol-Bristol, TN-VA Metropolitan Statistical Area	220	72.7	286
Kingston, NY Metropolitan Statistical Area	191	104.5	121
Knoxville, TN Metropolitan Statistical Area	444	66.5	310

(Continued)

Metropolitan Area	Complaints	Complaints Per 100,000 Population	Rank
Kokomo, IN Metropolitan Statistical Area	83	82.3	237
La Crosse, WI-MN Metropolitan Statistical Area	52	40.2	375
Lafayette, IN Metropolitan Statistical Area	187	100.7	133
Lafayette, LA Metropolitan Statistical Area	255	100.2	137
Lake Charles, LA Metropolitan Statistical Area	145	75.4	273
Lake Havasu City-Kingman, AZ Micropolitan Statistical Area	360	186.5	13
Lakeland, FL Metropolitan Statistical Area	784	139.6	47
Lancaster, PA Metropolitan Statistical Area	460	93.0	172
Lansing-East Lansing, MI Metropolitan Statistical Area	261	57.5	340
Laredo, TX Metropolitan Statistical Area	454	196.1	12
Las Cruces, NM Metropolitan Statistical Area	305	157.3	25
Las Vegas-Paradise, NV Metropolitan Statistical Area	2,398	134.9	55
Lawrence, KS Metropolitan Statistical Area	70	62.4	327
Lawton, OK Metropolitan Statistical Area	96	87.9	210
Lebanon, NH-VT Micropolitan Statistical Area	120	69.6	298
Lebanon, PA Metropolitan Statistical Area	167	131.6	62
Lewiston-Auburn, ME Metropolitan Statistical Area	77	71.6	292
Lexington-Fayette, KY Metropolitan Statistical Area	288	66.0	312
Lima, OH Metropolitan Statistical Area	66	62.4	328
Lincoln, NE Metropolitan Statistical Area	116	40.8	373
Little Rock-North Little Rock, AR Metropolitan Statistical Area	615	94.2	164
Logan, UT-ID Metropolitan Statistical Area	56	50.4	356
Longview, TX Metropolitan Statistical Area	210	103.3	127
Los Angeles-Long Beach-Santa Ana, CA Metropolitan Statistical Area	18,761	144.9	39
Louisville-Jefferson County, KY-IN Metropolitan Statistical Area	805	65.9	315
Lubbock, TX Metropolitan Statistical Area	237	90.7	192
Lumberton, NC Micropolitan Statistical Area	149	115.5	90
Lynchburg, VA Metropolitan Statistical Area	183	76.4	267
Macon, GA Metropolitan Statistical Area	362	157.9	24
Madera, CA Metropolitan Statistical Area	410	280.2	2
Madison, WI Metropolitan Statistical Area	271	49.9	358
Manchester-Nashua, NH Metropolitan Statistical Area	320	79.4	252
Manhattan, KS Micropolitan Statistical Area	71	67.0	305
Mansfield, OH Metropolitan Statistical Area	98	77.2	264
McAllen-Edinburg-Mission, TX Metropolitan Statistical Area	1,563	223.1	5
Medford, OR Metropolitan Statistical Area	157	79.7	248

(Continued)

Metropolitan Area	Complaints	Complaints Per 100,000 Population	Rank
Memphis, TN-MS-AR Metropolitan Statistical Area	1,457	114.3	94
Merced, CA Metropolitan Statistical Area	397	161.6	22
Meridian, MS Micropolitan Statistical Area	99	94.8	162
Miami-Fort Lauderdale-Miami Beach, FL Metropolitan Statistical Area	8,317	152.2	31
Michigan City-La Porte, IN Metropolitan Statistical Area	131	118.6	84
Midland, TX Metropolitan Statistical Area	110	88.4	207
Milwaukee-Waukesha-West Allis, WI Metropolitan Statistical Area	1,050	69.5	299
Minneapolis-St. Paul-Bloomington, MN-WI Metropolitan Statistical Area	2,243	70.6	293
Missoula, MT Metropolitan Statistical Area	89	87.8	211
Mobile, AL Metropolitan Statistical Area	321	79.4	253
Modesto, CA Metropolitan Statistical Area	749	146.2	36
Monroe, LA Metropolitan Statistical Area	155	90.0	195
Monroe, MI Metropolitan Statistical Area	258	166.4	18
Montgomery, AL Metropolitan Statistical Area	547	151.2	32
Morgantown, WV Metropolitan Statistical Area	95	82.5	235
Morristown, TN Metropolitan Statistical Area	120	90.3	194
Mount Vernon-Anacortes, WA Metropolitan Statistical Area	162	140.0	46
Muncie, IN Metropolitan Statistical Area	71	61.8	331
Muskegon-Norton Shores, MI Metropolitan Statistical Area	104	59.4	336
Myrtle Beach-Conway-North Myrtle Beach, SC Metropolitan Statistical Area	195	81.8	238
Napa, CA Metropolitan Statistical Area	404	302.6	1
Naples-Marco Island, FL Metropolitan Statistical Area	331	105.2	117
Nashville-Davidson--Murfreesboro, TN Metropolitan Statistical Area	1,061	72.9	284
New Bern, NC Micropolitan Statistical Area	142	120.5	81
New Haven-Milford, CT Metropolitan Statistical Area	895	105.9	114
New Orleans-Metairie-Kenner, LA Metropolitan Statistical Area	934	91.2	183
New York-Northern New Jersey-Long Island, NY-NJ-PA Metropolitan Statistical Area	21,090	112.1	100
Niles-Benton Harbor, MI Metropolitan Statistical Area	205	126.8	70
Norwich-New London, CT Metropolitan Statistical Area	218	82.8	234
Ocala, FL Metropolitan Statistical Area	355	112.3	99
Odessa, TX Metropolitan Statistical Area	119	93.4	169
Ogden-Clearfield, UT Metropolitan Statistical Area	401	80.6	243
Ogdensburg-Massena, NY Micropolitan Statistical Area	49	44.0	369
Oklahoma City, OK Metropolitan Statistical Area	1,039	88.6	203

(Continued)

Metropolitan Area	Complaints	Complaints Per 100,000 Population	Rank
Olympia, WA Metropolitan Statistical Area	243	103.5	126
Omaha-Council Bluffs, NE-IA Metropolitan Statistical Area	497	60.4	333
Orlando-Kissimmee, FL Metropolitan Statistical Area	2,586	130.3	63
Oshkosh-Neenah, WI Metropolitan Statistical Area	105	65.4	317
Ottawa-Streator, IL Micropolitan Statistical Area	108	70.0	294
Owensboro, KY Metropolitan Statistical Area	94	83.9	225
Oxnard-Thousand Oaks-Ventura, CA Metropolitan Statistical Area	1,231	153.9	27
Palm Bay-Melbourne-Titusville, FL Metropolitan Statistical Area	475	88.9	200
Panama City-Lynn Haven, FL Metropolitan Statistical Area	144	88.1	209
Parkersburg-Marietta-Vienna, WV-OH Metropolitan Statistical Area	74	45.8	365
Pascagoula, MS Metropolitan Statistical Area	211	138.4	48
Pensacola-Ferry Pass-Brent, FL Metropolitan Statistical Area	389	88.4	208
Peoria, IL Metropolitan Statistical Area	202	54.6	348
Philadelphia-Camden-Wilmington, PA-NJ-DE-MD Metropolitan Statistical Area	5,778	99.2	143
Phoenix-Mesa-Scottsdale, AZ Metropolitan Statistical Area	6,165	152.6	29
Pine Bluff, AR Metropolitan Statistical Area	92	88.8	202
Pittsburgh, PA Metropolitan Statistical Area	1,428	60.2	334
Pittsfield, MA Metropolitan Statistical Area	59	45.0	367
Port St. Lucie-Fort Pierce, FL Metropolitan Statistical Area	526	134.1	57
Portland-South Portland-Biddeford, ME Metropolitan Statistical Area	281	54.7	347
Portland-Vancouver-Beaverton, OR-WA Metropolitan Statistical Area	1,770	82.8	233
Pottsville, PA Micropolitan Statistical Area	169	114.7	93
Poughkeepsie-Newburgh-Middletown, NY Metropolitan Statistical Area	612	91.1	184
Prescott, AZ Metropolitan Statistical Area	366	175.9	17
Providence-New Bedford-Fall River, RI-MA Metropolitan Statistical Area	1,080	67.0	306
Provo-Orem, UT Metropolitan Statistical Area	381	80.3	245
Pueblo, CO Metropolitan Statistical Area	162	105.9	113
Punta Gorda, FL Metropolitan Statistical Area	239	154.8	26
Racine, WI Metropolitan Statistical Area	196	100.0	139
Raleigh-Cary, NC Metropolitan Statistical Area	910	91.5	180
Rapid City, SD Metropolitan Statistical Area	77	64.8	321

(Continued)

Metropolitan Area	Complaints	Complaints Per 100,000 Population	Rank
Reading, PA Metropolitan Statistical Area	398	99.2	142
Redding, CA Metropolitan Statistical Area	165	91.7	178
Reno-Sparks, NV Metropolitan Statistical Area	444	110.8	102
Richmond, VA Metropolitan Statistical Area	961	80.5	244
Riverside-San Bernardino-Ontario, CA Metropolitan Statistical Area	6,084	151.1	33
Roanoke, VA Metropolitan Statistical Area	221	74.9	278
Rochester, MN Metropolitan Statistical Area	88	49.0	361
Rochester, NY Metropolitan Statistical Area	640	61.8	330
Rockford, IL Metropolitan Statistical Area	344	98.8	147
Rocky Mount, NC Metropolitan Statistical Area	199	136.0	52
Roseburg, OR Micropolitan Statistical Area	113	107.5	109
Sacramento--Arden-Arcade--Roseville, CA Metropolitan Statistical Area	2,625	127.0	69
Saginaw-Saginaw Township North, MI Metropolitan Statistical Area	184	89.2	199
Salem, OR Metropolitan Statistical Area	377	98.0	150
Salinas, CA Metropolitan Statistical Area	503	122.6	76
Salisbury, MD Metropolitan Statistical Area	119	101.1	131
Salisbury, NC Micropolitan Statistical Area	218	160.0	23
Salt Lake City, UT Metropolitan Statistical Area	893	83.6	228
San Angelo, TX Metropolitan Statistical Area	79	74.7	279
San Antonio, TX Metropolitan Statistical Area	2,331	120.0	82
San Diego-Carlsbad-San Marcos, CA Metropolitan Statistical Area	3,509	119.3	83
San Francisco-Oakland-Fremont, CA Metropolitan Statistical Area	5,514	131.9	60
San Jose-Sunnyvale-Santa Clara, CA Metropolitan Statistical Area	2,241	125.4	71
San Luis Obispo-Paso Robles, CA Metropolitan Statistical Area	313	121.8	77
Santa Barbara-Santa Maria, CA Metropolitan Statistical Area	441	110.2	104
Santa Cruz-Watsonville, CA Metropolitan Statistical Area	383	153.4	28
Santa Fe, NM Metropolitan Statistical Area	175	122.9	75
Santa Rosa-Petaluma, CA Metropolitan Statistical Area	525	112.4	98
Sarasota-Bradenton-Venice, FL Metropolitan Statistical Area	569	83.3	230
Savannah, GA Metropolitan Statistical Area	290	90.6	193
Scranton--Wilkes-Barre, PA Metropolitan Statistical Area	429	77.9	260
Seaford, DE Micropolitan Statistical Area	158	87.6	213
Seattle-Tacoma-Bellevue, WA Metropolitan Statistical Area	2,976	91.2	182
Sebastian-Vero Beach, FL Metropolitan Statistical Area	186	143.0	41

(Continued)

Metropolitan Area	Complaints	Complaints Per 100,000 Population	Rank
Sheboygan, WI Metropolitan Statistical Area	68	59.3	337
Sherman-Denison, TX Metropolitan Statistical Area	119	100.4	135
Shreveport-Bossier City, LA Metropolitan Statistical Area	296	76.5	266
Sierra Vista-Douglas, AZ Micropolitan Statistical Area	209	163.6	20
Sioux City, IA-NE-SD Metropolitan Statistical Area	70	48.8	362
Sioux Falls, SD Metropolitan Statistical Area	82	38.5	378
South Bend-Mishawaka, IN-MI Metropolitan Statistical Area	463	145.6	37
Spartanburg, SC Metropolitan Statistical Area	240	88.5	205
Spokane, WA Metropolitan Statistical Area	340	76.1	269
Springfield, IL Metropolitan Statistical Area	119	57.7	339
Springfield, MA Metropolitan Statistical Area	587	85.5	219
Springfield, MO Metropolitan Statistical Area	329	80.8	241
Springfield, OH Metropolitan Statistical Area	183	129.0	65
St. Cloud, MN Metropolitan Statistical Area	77	42.1	372
St. George, UT Metropolitan Statistical Area	100	79.2	255
St. Joseph, MO-KS Metropolitan Statistical Area	95	77.7	261
St. Louis, MO-IL Metropolitan Statistical Area	2,100	75.1	277
State College, PA Metropolitan Statistical Area	94	66.7	307
Statesville-Mooresville, NC Micropolitan Statistical Area	209	142.9	42
Staunton-Waynesboro, VA Micropolitan Statistical Area	61	52.7	353
Stockton, CA Metropolitan Statistical Area	1,096	162.8	21
Sumter, SC Metropolitan Statistical Area	142	136.0	53
Syracuse, NY Metropolitan Statistical Area	428	65.8	316
Tallahassee, FL Metropolitan Statistical Area	322	95.7	157
Tampa-St. Petersburg-Clearwater, FL Metropolitan Statistical Area	2,713	100.6	134
Terre Haute, IN Metropolitan Statistical Area	145	86.2	217
Texarkana, TX-Texarkana, AR Metropolitan Statistical Area	129	95.9	155
Thomasville-Lexington, NC Micropolitan Statistical Area	322	206.1	10
Toledo, OH Metropolitan Statistical Area	514	78.6	257
Topeka, KS Metropolitan Statistical Area	205	89.6	197
Torrington, CT Micropolitan Statistical Area	261	137.3	50
Traverse City, MI Micropolitan Statistical Area	90	63.4	326
Trenton-Ewing, NJ Metropolitan Statistical Area	334	90.9	189
Tucson, AZ Metropolitan Statistical Area	1,422	150.3	34
Tulsa, OK Metropolitan Statistical Area	719	80.1	246
Tupelo, MS Micropolitan Statistical Area	105	79.6	250
Tuscaloosa, AL Metropolitan Statistical Area	148	74.5	280

(Continued)

Metropolitan Area	**Complaints**	**Complaints Per 100,000 Population**	**Rank**
Tyler, TX Metropolitan Statistical Area	193	99.2	144
Utica-Rome, NY Metropolitan Statistical Area	158	53.1	351
Valdosta, GA Metropolitan Statistical Area	115	91.0	186
Vallejo-Fairfield, CA Metropolitan Statistical Area	898	218.1	6
Victoria, TX Metropolitan Statistical Area	131	114.8	92
Vineland-Millville-Bridgeton, NJ Metropolitan Statistical Area	104	67.2	304
Virginia Beach-Norfolk-Newport News, VA-NC Metropolitan Statistical Area	1,310	79.4	254
Visalia-Porterville, CA Metropolitan Statistical Area	595	141.7	43
Waco, TX Metropolitan Statistical Area	158	69.9	295
Warner Robins, GA Metropolitan Statistical Area	151	118.4	85
Washington-Arlington-Alexandria, DC-VA-MD-WV Metropolitan Statistical Area	5,594	105.7	115
Waterloo-Cedar Falls, IA Metropolitan Statistical Area	63	38.8	376
Watertown-Fort Drum, NY Micropolitan Statistical Area	68	59.5	335
Wausau, WI Metropolitan Statistical Area	68	52.2	354
Weirton-Steubenville, WV-OH Metropolitan Statistical Area	107	85.5	220
Wenatchee, WA Metropolitan Statistical Area	109	102.1	129
Wheeling, WV-OH Metropolitan Statistical Area	74	50.2	357
Whitewater, WI Micropolitan Statistical Area	100	99.0	145
Wichita Falls, TX Metropolitan Statistical Area	145	99.6	140
Wichita, KS Metropolitan Statistical Area	491	82.9	231
Williamsport, PA Metropolitan Statistical Area	101	85.8	218
Willimantic, CT Micropolitan Statistical Area	165	141.2	45
Wilmington, NC Metropolitan Statistical Area	227	69.6	297
Winchester, VA-WV Metropolitan Statistical Area	127	106.8	112
Winston-Salem, NC Metropolitan Statistical Area	476	104.2	122
Wooster, OH Micropolitan Statistical Area	111	97.4	151
Worcester, MA Metropolitan Statistical Area	713	90.8	190
Yakima, WA Metropolitan Statistical Area	261	112.0	101
York-Hanover, PA Metropolitan Statistical Area	365	87.7	212
Youngstown-Warren-Boardman, OH-PA Metropolitan Statistical Area	454	77.4	263
Yuba City, CA Metropolitan Statistical Area	318	196.5	11
Yuma, AZ Metropolitan Statistical Area	336	179.1	15

[1] Ranking is based on the number of identity theft complaints per 100,000 inhabitants for each Metropolitan Area. This chart illustrates Metropolitan Areas (Metropolitan and Micropolitan Statistical Areas) with a population of one hundred thousand or more. Metropolitan Areas presented here are those defined by the Office of Management and Budget as of December 2005 and the population estimates are based on the 2006 U.S. Census table CBSA-EST2006-01.

In: Mass Marketing and Consumer Fraud...
Editor: Martin A. Parham
ISBN: 978-1-60692-793-9

Chapter 2

MASS-MARKETING FRAUD: A REPORT TO THE MINISTER OF PUBLIC SAFETY OF CANADA AND THE ATTORNEY GENERAL OF THE UNITED STATES, MARCH 2008*

Mass-Marketing Fraud Subgroup and Cross Border Crime Forum

INTRODUCTION

In April 1997, then-Prime Minister of Canada Jean Chrétien and then-President of the United States Bill Clinton directed the preparation of a joint study examining ways to counter the serious and growing problem of cross-border telemarketing fraud. In November 2007, a binational working group established for that purpose provided a report to the Prime Minister and the President that contains a detailed examination of the problem and a series of recommendations to improve both countries' responses to the problem.[1] Those recommendations included identification of telemarketing fraud as a serious crime; establishment of regional task forces to cooperate across the international border; coordination of strategies to control telemarketing fraud between both countries at agency, regional, and national levels; operation of an ongoing binational working group to provide overall coordination; and other recommendations to address information-gathering, evidence-sharing and mutual legal assistance, extradition, and public education and prevention.[2]

The 1997 Report became a general blueprint for coordinated binational actions against telemarketing fraud. In the ten years since the issuance of the 1997 Report, Canada and the United States have not only carried out all of the recommendations in that Report, but have made even greater strides in combating what is now termed mass-marketing fraud - i.e., fraud schemes that use mass communications methods, such as telemarketing, the Internet, and mass mailing to contact and communicate with large numbers of prospective victims and to obtain funds from victims.

---

* This is an edited, reformatted and augmented version of a Mass Marketing Fraud Subgroup and Cross Border Crime Forum publication dated March 2008.

This chapter has three purposes. First, it will describe the principal trends and developments since 2003 in four major types of crime associated with mass-marketing fraud (i.e., telemarketing fraud schemes, Internet fraud schemes, Nigerian fraud[3], and identity theft). Second, it will summarize the principal approaches that law enforcement in both countries have adopted since 2003 to combat mass-marketing fraud more effectively. Third, it will report on recommendations that this Subgroup made in 2003 as part of a binational action plan to combat mass-marketing fraud, and set out additional recommendations that address changes in the nature and types of mass-marketing fraud that have emerged since 2003.

SECTION I: MASS-MARKETING FRAUD IN CANADA AND THE UNITED STATES

For more than a decade, Canada and the United States have been actively combating the problem of mass-marketing fraud. Although it originally encompassed only cross-border telemarketing fraud, mass-marketing fraud affecting both countries has since expanded into a multifaceted problem that includes traditional telemarketing fraud, Internet fraud, Nigerian fraud, and identity theft. The 2006 joint Canada/United States Organized Crime Threat Assessment observed that identity theft, Internet fraud, and money laundering were among the financial crimes "that are growing in scale, scope, and sophistication."[4] Moreover, newer developments – including the dramatically increased use of counterfeit checks and money orders, and the substantial use of various payment mechanisms such as payment processors and money transfer businesses in connection with mass-marketing fraud schemes – have further complicated the tasks of law enforcement in mounting effective responses to cross-border mass-marketing fraud.

This Section of the report will discuss the principal trends and developments since 2003 in cross-border telemarketing fraud, Internet fraud, Nigerian fraud, and identity theft.

A. Telemarketing Fraud

1. Background

Telemarketing fraud is both the oldest and, in some respects, the most persistent form of mass-marketing fraud that Canada and the United States must combat. As the 2006 Canada/United States Organized Crime Threat Assessment noted, telemarketing fraud "continues to target both Canadian and US citizens."[5]

In the United States, a private non-profit entity, the National Consumers League (NCL) reported that in 2006 (the most recent year for which data are available) the ten leading types of telemarketing fraud were as listed below in Table I:[6]

Two observations about these data are in order. First, fake check schemes – in which victims are persuaded to deposit checks that later prove to be counterfeit into their bank accounts and to send the criminals a portion of the deposited check – not only were the leading type of complaint but also generated the highest average loss per victim. Second, lotteries and lottery clubs accounted for the second highest average loss, but constituted only

6 percent of the complaints, while prize and sweepstakes schemes were the second leading type of telemarketing scheme and generated the third highest average loss.

Table I. National Consumers League Fraud Center, 2006 Telemarketing Fraud Data

	Type of Scheme	Percentage of Complaints	Average Victim Loss
1.	Fake Check Schemes	31	$3,278
2.	Prize/Sweepstakes Schemes	26	$2,749
3.	Magazine Sales	8	$77
4.	Scholarships/Grants	6	$236
5.	Advance Fee Loans	6	$1,164
6.	Lotteries/Lottery Clubs	6	$3,189
7.	Credit Card Offers	4	$237
8.	Phishing	3	$387
9.	Work-at-Home Plans	1	$104
10.	Travel/Vacation	1	$812

Table II. Phonebusters 2005-2007 Fraud Complaint Data (Including Prize, Loan, Vacation and Other Schemes)

	2005	2006	2007
Canadian Attempts	11,306	10,830	14,433
Canadian Victims	4,608	4,192	4,124
Value of Canadian Loss Reported	$16,498,990.70	$24,532,680.04	$18,177,921.36
U.S. Attempts	10,668	13,350	9,069
U.S. Victims	12,214	10,908	8,684
Value of U.S. Loss Reported	$58,432,710.73	$48,830,098.19	$35,438,164.96
U.K. Attempts	32	16	14
U.K. Victims	115	47	56
Value of U.K. Loss Reported	$730,925.99	$1,296,538.41	$987,924.05
Other Countries/Unknown Attempts	186	76	72
Other Countries/Unknown Victims	169	87	177
Value of Other Countries/Unknown Losses Reported	$657,909.58	$1,383,452.12	$4,099,652.54
Total Fraud Attempts	22,192	24,272	23,588
Total Fraud Victims	17,106	15,234	13,041
Total Fraud Loss Reported	$76,320,537.00	$76,042,768.76	$58,703,662.91

With respect to these 2006 data, the NCL reported that the five leading locations of telemarketing fraud schemes that U.S. consumers reported were as follows: (1) Canada (30 percent); (2) Countries outside the United States and Canada (15 percent); (3) Florida (8 percent); (4) New York (7 percent); and (5) California (5 percent). The NCL also noted that foreign telemarketing fraud schemes targeting U.S. residents accounted for 45 percent of all complaints in 2006 – a substantial increase from 2006 (26 percent).[7]

In Canada, PhoneBusters, the Canadian Anti-fraud Call Center, reported the following data for various fraudulent solicitations from 2005 to 2007:[8]

Several observations about these data are in order. First, while the number of attempted fraud contacts with Canadian residents increased from 2006 to 2007, the number of actual Canadian victims remained virtually the same but the total amount of Canadian loss declined by one-third. Second, the numbers of U.S. attempted fraud contacts with U.S. residents and actual U.S. victims, as well as the total amount of U.S. loss, (as reported to PhoneBusters) all declined from 2006 to 2007. Third, the small number of attempted fraud contacts with U.K. residents and the total amount of U.K. loss declined slightly from 2006 to 2007. Fourth, the number of victims from other countries (or unknown locations), and the total amount of their loss, substantially increased from 2006 to 2007, as the number of victims more than doubled and the total loss nearly tripled.

2. Trends

In general, some features of cross-border telemarketing fraud, such as substantial reliance on money transfer businesses to receive proceeds from victims, have remained in use over the past several years. Other characteristics, however, have undergone substantial transformation since 2003, as described below:

a. Involvement of Organized Crime

The most far-reaching change in cross-border telemarketing fraud since 2003 is the substantial and growing involvement of Nigerian-led criminal rings in telemarketing fraud and other financial fraud, including Internet fraud schemes such as "phishing"[9] and various schemes that involve use of counterfeit checks.[10] Law enforcement authorities report that while they believe certain elements of traditional hierarchical organized crime groups continue to be involved in cross-border telemarketing fraud – particularly with respect to the provision of "leads" (i.e., names and related data of prior fraud victims), "protection"[11] of telemarketing-fraud rooms, and money laundering services – the number of Nigerian-led fraud operations has increased significantly in several major metropolitan areas of Canada, as they have in several West African countries and various European countries such as the Netherlands, Spain, and the United Kingdom. These Nigerian-led rings routinely use the services of multiple individuals in often elaborate and carefully conducted schemes, often performing specific functions in multiple countries, though they lack the hierarchical characteristics of various ethnic organized criminal groups in North America and Europe.

b. "Pitches" and Other Operational Features

For non-Nigerian criminal operations, many of the telemarketing fraud "pitches" (i.e., false or fraudulent stories and explanations for the criminals' requests or demands for payments by prospective victims) that were prevalent in the first part of this decade have continued to be extensively used in the last five years. These include fraudulent offers of prizes or sweepstakes or lottery winnings, fraudulent offers of "guaranteed" credit cards or loans, and so-called "business-to-business" schemes (i.e., offers of listings in nonexistent business directories, or of office-related supplies and products).[12] These schemes can be extraordinarily lucrative. For example, the co-owner of two telemarketing firms that operated in Montreal and Toronto and targeted exclusively U.S. companies with fraudulent business directory listings and other schemes was recently convicted at trial of violating ten counts of the Competition Act by making false or misleading representations through his firms. According to one estimate, the two firms were estimated to have had more than $70 million in sales.[13]

With the growing incursion of Nigerian-led fraud schemes based in Canada, law enforcement authorities have seen movement toward a wider variety of advance-fee schemes that are characteristic of Nigerian criminal rings. These include fraudulent solicitations that seek to persuade a prospective victim to deposit into the victim's personal bank account a check sent by the scheme to and wire-transfer a portion of the funds back to the control of the scheme. Victims routinely do so, only to find out at a later date that the checks are counterfeit and that they not only have lost the funds wired to the scheme but are liable to the bank where the check was deposited for the full face amount of the check.

Law enforcement authorities have noted that certain schemes operated by Nigerian criminal rings often use regular mail and email as the initial method of contacting victims, but then rely extensively on telephonic contact with a victim who had responded positively to the initial mail solicitation. As indicated above, some Nigerian-related schemes engage in identity theft through online techniques such as "phishing" to acquire victims' personal identifying and financial account data.

c. Concealment Techniques

One technique that law enforcement authorities report cross-border fraud schemes are increasingly using is the Voice over Internet Protocol (VoIP) technology. VoIP has been defined as

> a technology that allows you to make voice calls using a broadband Internet connection instead of a regular (or analog) phone line. Some VoIP services may only allow you to call other people using the same service, but others may allow you to call anyone who has a telephone number - including local, long distance, mobile, and international numbers. Also, while some VoIP services only work over your computer or a special VoIP phone, other services allow you to use a traditional phone connected to a VoIP adapter.[14]

Because VoIP services can allow the VoIP user to display to callers a telephone number different from the actual number at which the VoIP user is located, fraud schemes can mislead prospective victims into thinking that the location they are calling is in a different location (e.g., a Florida-based investment fraud scheme that falsely displays a telephone number in the 212 (New York City) area code, or a Toronto-based advance-fee scheme that falsely displays a telephone number in a non-Toronto area code). Law enforcement authorities have noticed the use of VoIP technology by major telemarketing fraud operations in Canada and Costa Rica that targeted U.S. victims.

d. Methods of Transmitting Funds

In general, the period from 2003 to 2008 saw a continuation of the trend towards having victims transmit their payments to fraud schemes by wire transfer, particularly the leading money-transfer businesses Western Union and MoneyGram. For example, in the United States, the National Consumers League reported that in 2006 wire transfer was by far the leading mode of payment in telemarketing schemes, accounting for 54 percent of all complaints that reported a mode of payment. The next three types of payment accounted for another 35 percent of complaints: (2) bank debits (14 percent); (3) checks (11 percent); and credit cards (10 percent).[15]

In the first several years of this decade, law enforcement authorities, particularly in Québec, noted that organized criminal group members in some cases had sought either to compromise or to threaten agents with money transfer services, to reduce the amount of record-keeping associated with receipt of funds transfers from fraud victims. Law enforcement authorities are now seeing that in some areas of Canada, members of Nigerian criminal rings, in order to avoid detection, are applying for and receiving Money Gram and Western Union franchises. These franchises are operated only as store fronts and are solely used for money laundering purposes rather than legitimate business activity.

B. Internet Fraud

1. Background

Since the creation of the World Wide Web, law enforcement authorities in North America have observed a wide variety of fraud schemes that use the Internet for various purposes, ranging from initial contact with prospective victims to receiving and laundering funds from victims. The most current U.S. statistical data regarding complaints about Internet fraud are available in a February 2008 report by the Federal Trade Commission (FTC). These data reflect Internet fraud-related complaints that the FTC received from 2005 through 2007, as shown below in Table III:[16]

Several aspects of these data deserve mention. While the total number of Internet-related fraud complaints in 2007 increased by nearly 8 percent since 2006, the total loss, average, and median amounts all decreased from 2006. At the same time, total losses reported in 2007 still exceed $525 million, an exceptional amount of reported financial loss for any type of fraud. In addition, because the average amount paid by victims of Internet-related fraud schemes (i.e., the total amount paid divided by the number of victims who reported the amounts paid) substantially exceeds the median amount paid in all three years, it appears that a number of large payments by victims is skewing the average amount paid in each of the three years. For example, in 2007, the complaint data indicate that 83 percent of those complaints who reported loss amounts reported amounts of $1,000 or less, while 12 percent (22,458) reported payments of $1,000 to $5,000 and another 4 percent (7,017) reported payments of more than $5,000.[18]

Table III. FTC 2005-2007 Internet Fraud-Related Complaint Data

	2005	2006	2007
Number of Complaints	197,085	205,269	221,226
Total Amounts of Loss Reported	$336,345,604	$590,494,777	$525,743,643
Average Amount Paid	$2,095	$3,332	$2,730
Median Amount Paid[17]	$342	$500	$395

2. *Trends*

In the United States, the FTC reported the following data showing changes with respect to methods of payments during the period 2005-2007, as shown below in Table IV:[19]

These data are noteworthy in several respects. First, payments by wire transfer continue to be the highest-dollar total of payments, even though the total amount of 2007 wire transfer payments declined from 2006 even as the number of complaints reporting such transfers increased by nearly 24 percent since 2006. Second, credit cards remained a distant second to wire transfer as a method of payment, but the amount of credit-card payments increased by 24 percent over 2006 and the average credit-card payment in 2007 ($2,070) increased by more than 8 percent over the average credit-card payment in2006. Third, from 2006 to 2007 there was substantial declines in both the total amounts of reported payments by checks ($60 million to nearly $18 million) and bank account debits (nearly $22 million to nearly $14 million), even though the number of complaints reporting such payments did not change significantly from one year to the next. Fourth, there was a substantial increase from 2006 to 2007 in the amounts of payments by money orders (more than $16 million to more than $25 million), even as the number of complainants reporting such payments decreased by nearly 24 percent.

Additional trend data are available from the Internet Crime Complaint Center (IC3), a partnership of the FBI and the National White Collar Crime Center. The IC3 reported the following data for complaints it received in 2006:

The total dollar loss from all referred cases of fraud was $198.44 million with a median dollar loss of $724.00 per complaint. This is up from $183.12 million in total reported losses in 2005. Other significant findings related to an analysis of referrals include:

- Internet auction fraud was by far the most reported offense, comprising 44.9% of referred complaints. Non-delivered merchandise and/or payment accounted for 19.0% of complaints. Check fraud made up 4.9% of complaints. Credit/debit card fraud, computer fraud, confidence fraud, and financial institutions fraud round out the top seven categories of complaints referred to law enforcement during the year.
- Of those individuals who reported a dollar loss, the highest median losses were found among Nigerian letter fraud ($5,100), check fraud ($3,744), and other investment fraud ($2,695) complainants.

Table IV. Methods of Payment Reported by Consumers to FTC For Internet-Related Fraud Complaints, 2005-2007 [Amounts (Number of Complaints)]

	2005	2006	2007
Bank Account Debit	$11,181,001 (6,153)	$21,792,498 (6,643)	$13,751,585 (6,653)
Cash/Cash Advance	$11,164,636 (1,039)	$7,648,293 (1,169)	$7,943,260 (1,216)
Check	$21,804,907 (3,437)	$60,119,725 (2,850)	$17,906,180 (2,577)
Credit Cards	$19,004,962 (12,208)	$24,736,839 (12,927)	$30,681,611 (14,822)
Money Order	$7 ,839,943 (3,997)	$16,661,396 (3,660)	$25,663,620 (2,962)
Telephone Bill	$96,364 (424)	$259,659 (429)	$112,452 (298)
Wire Transfer	$41,786,350 (5,557)	$91,623,738 (8,769)	$76,670,821 (10,857)

- Among perpetrators, 75.2% were male and half resided in one of the following states: California, New York, Florida, Texas, Illinois, Pennsylvania and Tennessee. The majority of reported perpetrators were from the United States. However, a significant number of perpetrators where also located in United Kingdom, Nigeria, Canada, Romania, and Italy.
- Among complainants, 61.2% were male, nearly half were between the ages of 30 and 50 and one-third resided in one of the four most populated states: California, Texas, Florida, and New York. While most were from the United States, IC3 received a number of complaints from Canada, Great Britain, Australia, India, and Germany.
- Recent high activity scams seen by IC3 include hit man scams, phishing attempts associated with spoofed sites, and counterfeit checking scams.[20]

In addition, the National Consumers League (NCL), reported that the top ten Internet fraud schemes reported to it in 2006 were as shown in Table V below.[21] Several aspects of these data are noteworthy. First, online investment schemes appear to have surged in 2006. Those schemes not only generated the highest average loss of the top ten Internet schemes in 2006, but were in the top ten for the first time in a decade.[22] Second, fake check scams generated the second-highest average loss, even though they represented only 11 percent of complaints to the NCL. Because many fake check schemes are conducted by West African criminal rings, it is possible that some of the rings conducting those schemes are also involved in the Nigerian money offers that generated other complaints.

Third, as with the telemarketing complaints to the NCL, wire transfers represented by far the largest single method of payment (45 percent) in the online fraud schemes reported to the NCL. Other methods of payment reported for these online fraud schemes included credit cards (20 percent); bank debit (9 percent); debit card (8 percent); money order (8 percent); check (5 percent); cashier's checks (2 percent); and cash (2 percent).[23] Finally, the five most frequent location of online fraud schemes reported to the NCL were (1) countries outside the United States and Canada (38 percent); (2) California (10 percent); (3) Florida and New York (6 percenttie); (5) Texas and Canada (4 percent - tie); and (7) Illinois (3 percent).[24]

Table V. NCL 2006 Internet Fraud Complaint Data

	Percentage of All Complaints	*Average Loss*
1. Auctions	34	$1,331
2. General Merchandise	33	$1,197
3. Fake Check Scams	11	$4,053
4. Nigerian Money Offers	7	$3,741
5. Lotteries/Lottery Clubs	4	$1,750
6. Advance Fee Loans	3	$1,515
7. Phishing	2	No losses reported
8. Prizes/Sweepstakes	1	$2,447
9. Internet Access Services	1	$920
10. Investments	1	$4,759

C. Nigerian Fraud

A third significant type of mass-marketing fraud that the 2003 Report identified was Nigerian fraud: i.e., schemes, typically conducted by loosely-knit criminal networks with Nigerian affiliations, that involve various types of fraudulent solicitations by mail, fax, telephone, and email. These solicitations include, for example, offers of bogus opportunities to assist African residents in laundering illegal proceeds or transferring other funds out of Africa. There is a consensus among North American, European, and Nigerian law enforcement experts on Nigerian fraud schemes that these schemes, regardless of the type of fraud scheme or location of their principal operations, are conducted by loose-knit criminal networks dominated by individuals with Nigerian nationality or Nigerian tribal or family relationships, though lower-level participants in the scheme may include individuals with other West African nationalities as well as non-African nationalities.

In the United States, while there are no aggregate statistical data on the number of U.S. residents who are contacted in some manner by these schemes, the FTC's 2008 Consumer Fraud and Identity Theft Complaint Data shows that "Foreign Money Offers" is the fourth largest complaint category, with 32,868 complaints in Consumer Sentinel (or 4% of complaint total). In Canada, PhoneBusters has compiled the following data for Nigerian letter fraud schemes during the period 2005 to 2007, as shown in Table VI:[25]

A few observations about these data are appropriate. The average reported loss in 2007 is nearly $35,000. This average loss is substantially higher than the 2006 average loss of nearly $16,000, even though the number of reporting Canadian victims in 2007 is substantially below the number of reporting victims in 2006. It is entirely possible that one or two of the reporting victims reported losses as high as hundreds of thousands or even more than one million dollars, and that one or two such reports could significantly skew the average loss upwards. At the same time, law enforcement authorities have observed that some victims of Nigerian fraud initially underreport their fraud losses, in part because they find it difficult to admit to the true magnitude of their losses even after deciding to report the fact of the fraud and the loss.

Establishing the true magnitude of losses in any particular Africa-related fraud scheme is therefore particularly difficult without substantial investigation. Nonetheless, law enforcement authorities in both countries have identified the growth of these Nigerian-led fraud operations are becoming a more substantial threat to consumers in both Canada and the United States.

Table VI. PhoneBusters 2005-2007 Nigerian Letter Scam Complaint Data

	2005	2006	2007
Canadian Victims	175	192	152
Total Amount of Loss Reported	$9,168,422.34	$3,056,355.18	$5,264,488.15

Table VII. PhoneBusters 2005-2007 Identity Theft Complaint Data

	2005	2006	2007
Canadians At Risk	731	730	311
Canadian Victims	12,859	13,221	4,633
Value of Loss Reported	$8,683,603.54	$15,734,254.69	$6,383,477.37

D. Identity Theft

1. Background

In the past five years, identity theft has become a form of crime that reaches into every corner of North America, and that affects individuals in every demographic segment as well as legitimate companies and financial institutions. Although law enforcement agencies typically regard identity theft as a crime distinct from mass-marketing fraud, some identity theft schemes rely on fraudulent and deceptive representations by criminals to deceive people into disclosing their personal and financial details.

In Canada, PhoneBusters reported the following data for Canadian identity theft for 2005 through 2007, as shown in Table VII:[26]

It is worth noting that according to identity theft complaints to PhoneBusters, both the numbers of Canadian victims and the total amount of Canadian loss attributable to identity theft sharply declined from 2006 to 2007.

In the United States, the FTC reported that in 2007, identity theft, as has been the case for several years, was the most frequently reported type of consumer fraud. Identity theft accounted for 255,627 complaints in 2005, 246,124 in 2006, and 258,427 in 2007.[27]

2. Trends and Developments in Identity Theft

At present, law enforcement agencies in both countries do not have comprehensive statistical data that would allow them to track all identity theft trends with precision. Available statistical and other data, however, have enabled law enforcement agencies in Canada and the United States to identify certain significant trends over the past five years.

a. Identity Theft Techniques

(1) *Phishing*

One significant identity theft technique for which there are substantial long-term statistical data is "phishing." Phishing is a generic term used to refer to criminals' creation and use of emails and websites designed to look like those of legitimate companies and financial institutions, as a means of persuading individuals to disclose valuable personal and financial data. The 2006 Canada/United States Organized Crime Threat Assessment described phishing scams as "one of the most significant and lucrative identity theft-related threats to Internet users."[28]

Statistical data from the Anti-Phishing Working Group (APWG), a industry association focused on eliminating identity theft and fraud stemming from phishing and email "spoofing,"indicate that there are four distinct trends in phishing since 2003:

- **Incidence and Prevalence of Phishing**. Phishing may be the form of identity theft affecting North America that has grown the most dramatically in the last five years. In January 2004, the APWG published its first report on the nascent problem of phishing. The APWG reported that during that month, 176 unique phishing attacks were reported. At the time, that number of phishing attacks was believed to be significant because it represented a 52 percent increase over the number reported in December 2003.[29]
  Since then, the incidence and prevalence of phishing have grown vastly beyond what anyone in the public or private sector could have foreseen. In November 2007, the APWG received 28,074 unique phishing reports and found 23,630 unique phishing sites being hosted worldwide.[30] Moreover, phishing websites are being hosted in numerous countries, including the United States and various nations in Asia and Europe. In November 2007, the APWG reported that the top ten countries hosting phishing sites were: (1) China (24.21 percent); (2) United States (23.85 percent); (3) India (9.39 percent); (4) Russian Federation (8.06 percent); (5) Thailand (4.64 percent); (6) Romania (3.53 percent); (7) Germany (3.41 percent); (8) Republic of Korea (2.42 percent); (9) United Kingdom (1.47 percent); and (1) France (1.47 percent).[31]

- **Targeting of Industry Sectors**. Over time, the focus of phishing operations has consistently been on the financial services industry, but has now become almost exclusively on that industry. In January 2004, the APWG reported that 40 percent of phishing attacks involved the "hijacking" (misuse) of corporate brands in the financial sector, although certain major e-commerce companies such as eBay initially were the targets of a comparatively substantial number of phishing attacks.[32] By contrast, in November 2004, the APWG reported that in that single month, 178 distinct corporate brands had been "hijacked" in phishing attacks – the largest number of "hijacked" brands that it had ever recorded in a single month – and that 93.8 percent of all phishing attacks that month were directed at the financial services sector.[33] The APWG also reported that in November 2007, it noted "a substantial uptick in the number of Middle East and European financial services companies being targeted, . . . in addition to large US-based banking institutions and credit unions."[34]

- **Targeting of Specific Individuals**. One trend that law enforcement and information security analysts observed over the past five years has been the increased use of phishing attacks targeted at specific groups of individuals. This technique, sometimes called "spear-phishing," is intended to increase the percentage of individuals to whose data the criminals can gain access.
  Recently, the APWG reported that the number of unique phishing reports in November 2007 actually represented a decrease of more than 10,600 from the preceding month. Analysts attributed this decrease, in part, to "eCrime gangs' increasing focus on targeted phishing attacks against key executives to secure credentials for thefts against corporate assets."[35] In particular, analysts were seeing reports that company executives were receiving "specially targeted emails that attempt to do two things: 1) Install malware [malicious code] to give the phisher

access to the corporations' systems and 2) Gain access to the corporations' bank accounts."[36]

- **Use of Malicious Code.** In January 2004, the APWG reported that "[t]he majority of phishing attacks use a link to a website as their 'call to action', although a few attacks ask the recipient to download a file (that generally contains a virus or Trojan program [i.e., a Trojan horse program, which appears to have a benign function but actually contains some form of malicious computer code])."[37] In these few instances, the APWG, added,

> A small number of phishing attacks [i.e., 5] include a Trojan attachment in the message that recipients are encouraged to download and run. These Trojans generally contain keylogger programs that silently monitor the victim's computer for patterns of keystrokes that look like credit card numbers or social security numbers, or for new windows that open containing the name of a bank or credit card company. The program captures the typed information to a text file, and then uses a built-in email system to send the contents to an email dropbox for collection.[38]

By November 2007, APWG data indicate that the use of phishing-based Trojan horses and keyloggers has become a principal weapon in the phishing arsenal. In that month, the APWG found 3,500 Uniform Resource Locators (URLs)[39] on which malicious code applications that seek to obtain computer users' passwords were found.[40] The APWG also found that the top ten countries with websites hosting either phishing-based keyloggers or Trojan downloaders that downloads a keylogger were: (1) United States (68.93 percent): (2) Russian Federation (13.88 percent); (3) China (7.88 percent); (4) Republic of Korea (1.77 percent); (5) United Kingdom (1.67 percent); (6) Poland (1.53 percent); (7) Germany (1.38 percent); (8) France (1.13 percent); (9) Morocco (0.94 percent); and (10) Romania (0.89 percent).[41]
In addition, in November 2007 the APWG found 338 unique password-stealing malicious code applications. This number represents a slight decrease from the number of unique password-stealing malicious code applications in October 2007 (359), but is still the highest number of such applications in a single month since January 2007 (345).[42]
The APWG also reported that it was observing a high increases in "traffic redirectors" (i.e., malicious code that is designed to redirect an Internet user's network traffic to a location where it was not intended to go). The highest volume of these traffic redirectors, according to the APWG, is in malicious code that modifies a user's DNS (i.e., Domain Name System) server settings or hosts file to redirect either certain specific DNS lookups or all DNS lookups to a fraudulent DNS server. The fraudulent server replies with valid responses for most domains, but modifies the name server response to direct the user to certain fraudulent sites (e.g., phishing websites designed to look like the financial institutions where the user does his or her banking). As the APWG explains, "[t]his is particularly effective because the attackers can redirect any of the users requests at any time and the end-users have very little indication that this is happening as they could be typing in the address on their own and not following an email or Instant Messaging lure."[43]

Each of these four trends is of substantial concern to corporate entities and law enforcement agencies in both Canada and the United States. The latter trend, the increased use of malware and infection of websites, is a particular source of concern. Consistent with the APWG findings, one leading information security vendor recently reported that it was seeing 6,000 new infected webpages every day. Moreover, it indicated that less than 20 percent of these websites were hacker sites (i.e., sites crated with malicious intent); 83 percent were legitimate websites that an unauthorized third party had compromised.[44]

In response to the dramatic growth of phishing attacks, numerous financial institutions' websites in Canada and the United States now include specific warnings to banking customers about phishing, as well as guidance on how to report possible phishing attacks.[45] Law enforcement also increasingly includes warnings about phishing on websites and in special online reports to the general public.[46] In addition, both financial institutions and law enforcement agencies issues special advisories to the public when specific Phishing attacks are being directed at those institutions or agencies.[47]

(2) Other Identity Theft Techniques

Law enforcement authorities in both countries have observed that criminals use a wide variety of identity theft techniques, ranging from high-tech approaches such as phishing to low-tech approaches. Here are some of the more prominent techniques seen in both countries:[48]

- **"Dumpster Diving."** One of the simplest identity theft techniques that continues to be used in some locations is "dumpster diving": i.e., the retrieval of discarded documents, such as payment receipts or bank statements, from trash receptacles and dumpsters.

- **Employee/Insider Theft or Compromise of Data**. Employees in companies, financial institutions, or government agencies may steal or share sensitive personal data from worksites and use it themselves or sell those data to or share it with outsiders.

- **"Shoulder Surfing."** In public areas such as airports, ATM machines, and hotels, criminals will stand near telephone banks or ATM machines that consumers are using and try to see or hear any valuable data that the consumers are using (e.g., credit-card numbers or PIN codes for ATMs).

- **"Skimming."** Skimming may be considered a high-tech variant of shoulder surfing, in which criminals use electronic devices known as "skimmers" to capture the data on the magnetic stripes on the backs of payment cards. There are two principal types of skimmers currently in use: hand-held and non-portable. Hand-held skimmers are used by service workers in various types of retail businesses such as bars and restaurants. When a customer gives the worker his or her payment card, the worker can swipe the card through the legitimate business's swipe-card machine, then swipe the same card through the hand-held skimmer and provide the skimmer and all its captured data at a later date to other criminals. When a non-portable skimmer is mounted over the card slot on an ATM machine, the customer unwittingly sets the skimming process in motion by dipping his card into the slot. The criminals' skimmer reads the customer's magnetic stripe data first, then the legitimate financial institution's card-reader technology recognizes the customer's card and PIN number and effects the transaction. To capture the PIN number, the criminals sometimes use pinhole cameras mounted near the ATM's keypad so that the criminals can see and record the PIN numbers as ATM customers type in the numbers.[49]

- **Theft of Payment Cards and Documents from Personal Areas**. Identity thieves often resort to simple techniques, including theft of wallets or purses from places over which individuals cars and fitness centers and theft of incoming or outgoing mail. Incoming mail may include preapproved credit-card offers, which the identity theft can use to apply for cards in others' names and change the delivery address so the identity theft victim never receives any mail that would alert him to the issuance of cards that he did not request. Outgoing mail may include checks and payment invoices that the criminal can use to obtain access to a victim's bank or financial accounts.

b. Uses of Others' Identifying Data

As indicated earlier, criminals can use stolen or fraudulently obtained personal data in numerous ways to commit fraud and conceal their true identities, while falsely throwing suspicion on the victims whose data they have wrongly used. As the Royal Canadian Mounted Police have noted, once an identity thief has obtained a victim's data, he "can take over the victim's financial accounts, open new bank accounts, transfer bank balances, apply for loans, credit cards and other services, purchase vehicles, take luxury vacations, and so on."[50]

One significant trend in the online use of identity theft victims' data is the creation of "botnets" (i.e., networks of computers over which a criminal has taken control through hacking of those computers or introduction of malicious code into those computers). Once a criminal has amassed a botnet, he can use computers in that botnet to carry out a wide range of activity, such as emailing large volumes of spam to prospective victims, conducting denial-of-service attacks, disseminating malicious code, and supporting phishing attacks.[51] A number of information security experts affiliated with the SANS Institute, a leading information security training organization, concluded that the increasing sophistication and effectiveness of botnets will be one of the top online security threats in 2008.[52]

SECTION II: THE BINATIONAL RESPONSE TO MASS-MARKETING FRAUD, 2004-2008

Since the 2003 report, Canada and the United States have continued to provide vigorous support for a binational response to the increasingly varied problem of mass-marketing fraud. This Section of the Report will review changes in each country's significant substantive and procedural laws, task forces and strategic partnerships devoted to mass-marketing fraud, approaches to public education and prevention measures, and

A. Substantive and Procedural Laws

1. Canada

Since 2003, the most substantial proposed change in Canadian law pertinent to mass-marketing fraud involves identity theft. Recognizing that identity theft has become a fast-growing problem throughout North America, in November 2007 the Canadian Minister of Justice and Attorney General of Canada Rob Nicholson tabled legislation in the Canadian Parliament that would make it a crime to obtain, possess or traffic in other people's identity information if it is to be used to commit a crime.

The essential purpose and features of the proposed legislation are as follows:

> The misuse of another person's identity information, generally referred to as identity fraud, is covered by current offences in the *Criminal Code*, such as personation and forgery. But the preparatory steps of collecting, possessing and trafficking in identity information are generally not captured by existing offences. The proposed legislation would create three new offences directly targeting aspects of the identity theft problem, all subject to five-year maximum sentences:

- obtaining or possessing identity information with intent to use it to commit certain crimes;
- trafficking in identity information with knowledge of or recklessness as to its intended use in the commission of certain crime; and
- unlawfully possessing and trafficking in government-issued identity documents.

Additional *Criminal Code* amendments would create new offences of fraudulently redirecting or causing redirection of a person's mail, possessing a counterfeit Canada Post mail key and possessing instruments for copying credit card information, in addition to the existing offence of possessing instruments for forging credit cards.

Moreover, a new power would also be added permitting the court to order, as part of a sentence, that an offender be required to pay restitution to a victim of identity theft or identity fraud where the victim has incurred expenses related to rehabilitating their identity, such as the cost of replacement cards and documents and costs in relation to correcting their credit history.[53]

2. United States

One significant piece of U.S. legislation affecting mass-marketing fraud that was enacted since 2003 is the U.S. SAFEWEB Act.[54] This legislation provides the FTC with a number of significant sources of authority relating to cross-border fraud enforcement, including the following:

- It authorizes the FTC to disclose certain privileged or confidential information to foreign law enforcement agencies;
- It authorizes the FTC, upon written request, to provide investigative assistance to a foreign law enforcement agency that states it is investigating or enforcing proceedings against violations of laws prohibiting fraudulent or deceptive commercial practices or other practices substantially similar to practices prohibited

by laws administered by the FTC, other than federal antitrust laws, without requiring that the conduct identified constitute a violation of U.S. laws;

- It directs the FTC to (1) transmit to the Attorney General evidence of a violation of federal criminal law by any domestic or foreign person, partnership, or corporation, and (2) ensure, with respect to memoranda of understanding and international agreements, that material obtained from foreign law enforcement agencies may be used for investigation, prosecution, or prevention of U.S. criminal law violations;
- It authorizes the FTC to designate its attorneys to assist the Attorney General with litigation in foreign courts and to reimburse the Attorney General for the retention of foreign counsel for such litigation on matters in which the FTC has an interest;
- It specifies conditions under which an FTC-designated custodian is authorized to share certain compelled or confidential material with foreign law enforcement agencies that certify that the material will be maintained in confidence and will be used only for official law enforcement purposes, and exempts from public disclosure requirements of the Freedom of Information Act any material received by the FTC from foreign sources in the course of an investigation; and
- It authorizes the FTC to (1) retain employees of foreign government agencies on a temporary basis; (2) detail FTC employees to work for foreign agencies; (3) under the Right to Financial Privacy Act of 1978, share information with specified financial and market regulators; and (4) accept payment from a domestic or foreign law enforcement agency for FTC expenses and unconditional gifts, donations, bequests of property, and voluntary services.[55]

In addition, the United States, like Canada, is seeking additional legislation relating to identity theft. In April 2007, as part of a comprehensive national strategy for combating identity theft,[56] the President's Identity Theft Task Force recommended a number of changes in federal criminal law, including the following:

- Amending federal criminal restitution statutes to ensure that identity theft victims can recover for the value of the time they have spent in trying to remediate the harms they suffered;
- Amending the federal identity theft offense[57] and aggravated identity theft offense[58] to ensure that identity thieves who misappropriate information belonging to corporations and organizations can be prosecuted;
- Adding new crimes to the list of predicate offenses for aggravated identity theft;
- Amending the federal criminal statute pertaining to theft of electronic data[59] by eliminating the current requirement that the information must have been stolen through interstate communications;
- Penalizing creators and distributors of malicious spyware and keylogging software by amending the federal statute pertaining to theft of electronic data; and
- Amending the federal cyber-extortion statute[60] to cover additional types of cyber-extortion.[61]

This proposed legislation is now under active consideration in the U.S. Congress.

B. Task Forces and Strategic Partnerships

One of the cornerstones of the binational response to mass-marketing fraud over the past decade has been the establishment of binational task forces and strategic partnerships dedicated to combating mass-marketing fraud. Since 1998, when the first of these binational task forces, Project COLT in Montreal, was established, both countries have now set up six regional task forces and strategic partnerships: Project COLT; the Toronto Strategic Partnership; Project Emptor (Vancouver); the Alberta Partnership (Alberta); the Atlantic Provinces; and the Vancouver Strategic Alliance.

Each of these task forces and partnerships includes representatives of multiple Canadian and U.S. law enforcement agencies. Agencies represented on one or more of the task forces and strategic partnerships include the British Columbia Business Practices and Consumer Protection Authority, the City of Montreal Police Service, the Competition Bureau Canada, the Department of Homeland Security (Immigration & Customs Enforcement), the FBI, the FTC, the Ontario Ministry of Consumer and Commercial Relations, the Ontario Provincial Police, the Royal Canadian Mounted Police, the Sûreté du Québec, the Toronto Police Service, the United Kingdom Office of Fair Trading, the U.S. Attorney's Offices for the Central District of California and the Southern District of Illinois, and the U.S. Postal Inspection Service. These task forces and strategic partnerships continue to play a critical role in combating cross-border mass-marketing fraud, with respect not only to coordinated enforcement actions (see below) but also to public education and prevention measures and disruption of criminal operations.

C. Consumer Reporting and Information-Sharing Systems

1. Canada

In Canada, one vital resource for consumer reporting and information-sharing on mass-marketing fraud is PhoneBusters, the national Canadian Anti-fraud Call Center. PhoneBusters is managed

> on a tripartite basis by the Ontario Provincial Police, the Royal Canadian Mounted Police (RCMP) and the Competition Bureau Canada. PhoneBusters plays a key role in educating the public about specific fraudulent telemarketing pitches. The call centre also plays a vital role in the collection and dissemination of victim evidence, statistics, documentation and tape recordings which are made available to outside law enforcement agencies.[62]

PhoneBusters has been providing, and continues to provide, an important resource, both for consumers who wish to report telemarketing fraud, Nigerian fraud, or identity theft and for Canadian and U.S. law enforcement agencies that can draw on the information for analytical and investigative purposes.

Another highly valuable resource with respect to cross-border fraud, including Internet-related fraud, is the RCMP-established initiative known as Reporting Economic Crime On-Line (RECOL). RECOL involves an integrated partnership between international, federal, and provincial law enforcement agencies and with regulators and private commercial entities that have a legitimate investigative interest in receiving copies of complaints of economic crime. RECOL also provides real-time data pertaining to current fraud trends, as well as support for education, prevention, and awareness of economic crime.[63]

A third system that has been valuable for cross-border fraud cooperation is CANSHARE. CANSHARE is

> an internet-based information-sharing system developed by and for the use of federal and provincial consumer law enforcement agencies. By reducing duplication and increasing the speed and efficiency of information exchange between jurisdictions, [it] enables consumer law enforcement agencies to effectively allocate resources resulting in enhanced consumer protection programs. [It] also allows jurisdictions to monitor and analyze marketplace trends, identify and locate alleged wrongdoers and issue alerts warning of possible deceptive practices in the marketplace.[64]

Since being launched in 1998, CANSHARE was implemented by the federal government, all provinces, and two territories (i.e., theYukon and Northwest Territories).[65]

2. United States

For complaints about all types of consumer fraud, the principal national mechanism for receiving complaints and making complaint data available to law enforcement continues to be Consumer Sentinel. Consumer Sentinel is a complaint database that the FTC has maintained since 1997. Consumer Sentinel collects information about consumer fraud and identity theft from the FTC and over 125 other organizations and makes those data available to law enforcement partners across the United States and around the world for use in their investigations. The Sentinel database now includes more than 4.3 million complaints.[66] Complaints about identity theft filed with the FTC are accessible through the FTC's Identity Theft Data Clearinghouse.

For complaints about Internet-related crime, another vital resource for law enforcement and the public is the Internet Crime Complaint Center (IC3). IC3 is a partnership of the FBI and a nonprofit private-sector entity, the National White Collar Crime Center. IC3 takes and analyzes online complaints from the public and provides a central referral mechanism for law enforcement agencies at the state, national, and international levels. IC3 also provides periodic warnings to the public about specific types of online crime.[67]

Since the 2003 report, another initiative that can be of substantial value in mass-marketing fraud investigations is the National Cyber-Forensics and Training Alliance (NCFTA). The NCFTA is a nonprofit organization that provides a neutral collaborative venue where critical confidential information about cyber incidents can be shared discreetly, and where resources can be shared among industry, academia and law enforcement.[68] This unique partnership has been of substantial assistance to multiple federal law enforcement agencies in pursuing complex fraud investigations that involve online activity by criminals. For example, in connection with the 2005 Hurricane Katrina that devastated much of the U.S. Gulf Coast, the NCFTA provided critical assistance in reviewing large quantities of computer-related data to identify websites that potentially were engaging in fraudulent solicitations fo funds for Katrina victims.

D. Enforcement Accomplishments

1. Telemarketing Fraud

Since 2003, the various binational task forces and strategic partnerships, as well as their participating agencies, have brought a number of significant criminal and civil enforcement actions directed at cross-border telemarketing fraud. Here are some examples of those actions:

- *U.S. v. Bellini et al. (C.D. Cal., indictment filed December 19, 2007)*. In this case, on December 19, 2007, 22 defendants were indicted on federal fraud-related criminal charges for their roles in an extensive Montreal-based cross-border telemarketing fraud scheme. Members of the fraud operation allegedly

> contacted victims, the majority of whom were elderly, and falsely informed them that they had won large sums of money in a lottery or sweepstakes. The telemarketers allegedly told the victims that they would have to pay various fees or taxes – and in at least one case, money to rent an armored car that would be used to deliver sweepstakes winnings – to obtain their winnings. However, the indictment charges, none of the victims had won any money or would receive any money from the telemarketing organization. All of the money sent by victims to pay for the alleged fees was used by the various defendants for their own enjoyment.[69]

One of the defendants, the organizer and leader of the telemarketing organization, allegedly was responsible for obtaining equipment and facilities necessary for the operation of the organization, obtaining "leads" (i.e., listings of victim identifying and contact information) for his telemarketers, obtaining and providing cellular telephones for telemarketers' use, arranging for training of new members of the organization, bringing telemarketers together to "pitch" victims, providing for the collection of money that the victims sent, converting the checks obtained as a result of the organization's fraudulent activities into Canadian dollars, and distributing those funds to himself and other members of the organization. Other members of the organization allegedly made the actual phone calls to victims. Five of the defendants allegedly operated money transfer stores, specifically Western Union and MoneyGram, where some of the victims were instructed to wire money. With these contacts at the money transfer outlets, members of the organization could shield their identities by directing the victims to wire money to aliases, such as "Glen Ross."[70]

The indictment was the direct result of an eight-month investigation by Project COLT. In the course of that investigation, nearly 200 police officers in Canada conducted approximately 50 searches, primarily in the Montreal region, and the FTC contacted nearly 400 U.S. consumers to obtain victim declarations. Canadian authorities also arrested twenty of the 22 defendants later charged in the U.S. indictment. Eighty percent of the transactions reportedly were completed through money transfer sites based in Montreal. Law enforcement authorities estimated that the organization, which primarily conducted fraudulent lottery schemes and fraudulent offers of loans and grants, had been grossing between $5 million and $10 million annually since 2003.[71]

- *U.S. v. Okuomose (C.D. Cal., arrested Nov. 6, 2007)/FTC v. B.C. Ltd. 0763496, d.b.a. Cash Corner Services, Inc. Et al., Civil Action No. C07-1755 RSM (W.D. Wash., preliminary injunction entered November 13, 2007).* In this joint investigation by Project EMPTOR, a British Columbia resident was arrested by RCMP officers pursuant to a provisional arrest warrant based on a criminal complaint filed in U.S. District Court in Los Angeles. The defendant was wanted in connection with his involvement in a fraudulent lottery scheme victimizing U.S. residents that he operated under the name "Cash Corner Services" in British Columbia.

According to the complaint, the scheme was carried out by mailing letters advising victims they were lottery winners. The letters instructed victims that, in order to receive their lottery winnings, a fee was required. The complaint alleges that counterfeit checks were also enclosed with each letter which victims were instructed to use to help pay the required fees. Contact numbers listed on the correspondence would connect victims to telemarketers who confirmed that the victim had won the money, but that a fee was required in order to successfully retrieve the funds. Some victims did not receive a letter but only telephone calls from telemarketers who convinced them to send money to the lottery companies, according to the complaint. Victims were asked to send fees ranging from approximately a few thousand dollars to $24,000. After sending the money, victims attempted to deposit their checks and learned that the checks were worthless. No victims interviewed to date have received any money promised to them.[72]

In parallel civil actions, the FTC filed a civil action against the defendant, a relative of the defendant, Cash Corner Services, and another Canadian company, charging them with violations of the Federal Trade Commission Act and the FTC Telemarketing Sales Rule, and obtained a preliminary injunction. In addition, the British Columbia Business Practices and Consumer Protection Authority filed civil actions against the defendants, seeking to freeze their Canadian-based assets.[73]
It should be noted that the FTC staff used provisions of the U.S. SAFEWEB Act to assist Canadian enforcement agencies by sharing key information obtained in the FTC's investigation for use in the related Canadian law enforcement investigation.[74]

- *U.S. v. Porcelli (S.D. Ill., sentenced October 29, 2007).* In this case, on October 29, 2007, the defendant was sentenced to13 years imprisonment for his role in a telemarketing fraud scheme that defrauded individuals throughout the United States of approximately $12 million. The scheme, which targeted people previously rejected for credit cards with fraudulent credit-card offers, operated out of Florida and Utah and utilized U.S. outbound call centers in seven U.S. states; outbound call centers in Grenada, St. Lucia, and St. Vincent; an outbound call center in Toronto, Canada; and outbound call centers in India.[75]
- *Mass-Marketing Fraud Searches (Montreal, October 9, 2007).* On October 9, 2007, representatives of Project COLT conducted a number of searches in Montreal, in connection with a telemarketing fraud operation that reportedly victimized approximately 1,500 people. The operation's dialers used several pitches, including (1) selling first-aid kits to businesses under the false pretenses that they represented a federal health agency and that businesses were required to have such kits on their premises; (2) selling paper products in the guise of an office supplies dealer; and (3)

promoting sales of business listings in business directories, but failing to include those listings in the directories that were delivered. Victims of the scheme were principally small- and medium-sized businesses in Canada, the United States, and Europe.[76]

- *U.S. v. Kimoto (S.D. Ill., indictment filed June 20, 2007).* In this case, on June 20, 2007, a St, George, Utah and Las Vegas resident was indicted on various federal offenses arising out of an alleged telemarketing fraud scheme that fraudulently offered credit cards to individuals who previously had been turned down for credit cards. The indictment alleges that the scheme operated out of Utah and utilized a network of U.S. outbound call centers that the defendant organized in seven U.S. states; Caribbean outbound call centers in Grenada, St. Lucia, and St. Vincent; an outbound call center in Toronto, Canada; and outbound call centers in India. The indictment alleges that the scheme victimized more than 300,000 consumers throughout the United States, in an amount of approximately $43 million.[77] The defendant and his companies had previously been the subject of an FTC enforcement action that resulted in, among other things, judicial imposition of a receivership and a monetary judgment of $106 million against the defendant and one of his companies.[78]
- *U.S. v. Brown and Love (W.D.N.Y., guilty pleas entered March 29, 2007).* In this case, two Las Vegas residents pleaded guilty to federal criminal charges involving laundering the proceeds of illegal telemarketing activity in Canada. According to the U.S. Attorney's Office that prosecuted the case, in April 2004 one of the defendants met an individual online who identified herself as "Missy Young" of Ontario, Canada. "Young" (a false name) told that defendant that she and others in Canada were involved in telemarketing activities, and needed people in the United States to open bank accounts through which the proceeds of the telemarketing could be processed and sent back up to Canada. Between June 2004 and January 2005, the first defendant opened seven bank accounts at various banks, using various business names. That defendant enlisted the other defendant to open another two bank accounts. During this same period, the first defendant transferred and transmitted approximately $802,000 in U.S. funds to the telemarketers in Canada, including "Young," through wire transfers to bank accounts controlled by the telemarketers in the United States and Canada. The telemarketers also obtained funds from these bank accounts through ATM withdrawals made in the United States and in Canada. During the same period, and in the same manner, the second defendant transferred and transmitted approximately $630,700 in U.S. funds from her accounts to the telemarketers in Canada.

  The underlying telemarketing activity in Canada involved illegal schemes to obtain money by means of false and fraudulent pretenses and representations. Telemarketers in Canada allegedly contacted U.S. citizens and sold them a product or service for approximately $300. Based on the alleged sale, the telemarketers in Canada would create a "preauthorized draft check" and deposit it into one of the bank accounts that the defendants opened. It was part of the telemarketing fraud scheme that the personal and bank data put on the "preauthorized draft checks" – including the account holder's name, address, checking account number and bank routing number, -- was obtained through fraud, in that a large percentage of the checks were generated without the knowledge or permission of the person fraudulently identified as the "purchaser."[79]

2. Internet Fraud

The following are examples of cross-border Internet fraud prosecutions:

- *U.S. v. Hendricks (D. Ore., sentenced February 25, 2007).* In this case, on February 25, 2007, a Florida man was sentenced to six years imprisonment after pleading guilty to several federal criminal offenses relating to his role as the head of an investment fraud business which took in approximately $13 million from more than 1,500 victims throughout the United States and Canada. The defendant admitted that he used a company he and another individual had formed, Pacific Achievements International (PAI), to solicit investment funds through false statements and promises, primarily through the Internet. He falsely represented to investors that PAI would be a network marketing business and promised investors that if they invested with PAI, they would be sent a fast start bonus and significant profits.
  Based upon these false promises and representations, investors transferred more than $13 million into PAI bank accounts in Oregon, Washington, and Florida, that the defendant and another individual controlled. The defendant and another PAI promoter diverted more than $2 million in PAI money to support their personal livestyles, including the use of $1.6 million for the purchase of personal residences in Florida and Washington. Knowing that PAI was not generating any income, the defendant and another PAI promoter tried to recover funds by unsuccessfully investing PAI money in high yield investment scams in Beirut, Lebanon, the Bahamas, Nevada and Texas. They lost $2.7 million in PAI money in these other scams. The defendant ultimately pleaded guilty to conspiracy to commit mail and wire fraud, wire fraud, and failing to file a U.S. income tax return.[80]
- *U.S. v. Kraser (S.D. Fla., sentenced May 7, 2006).* In this case, a defendant was sentenced to 21 months in prison for fraudulently soliciting charitable donations supposedly intended for Hurricane Katrina relief. According to the indictment, the defendant falsely claimed in online conversations, and on a website at www.AirKatrina.com, that he was piloting flights to Louisiana to provide medical supplies to the areas affected by Hurricane Katrina and to evacuate children and others in critical medical condition. He also claimed that he had organized a group of Florida pilots to assist him in his supposed relief efforts.[81] In only two days, the defendant collected approximately $40,000 from 49 people in the United States, Canada, Mexico, Europe, and Hong Kong, with one contributor donating $20,000.[82]

3. Nigerian Fraud

As indicated above, Nigerian-led fraud operations are becoming a more substantial threat to consumers in both Canada and the United States. Recent significant law enforcement actions relating to Nigerian fraud operations include the following:

- *U.S. v. Anisiobi et al. (E.D.N.Y., guilty pleas entered January 30, 2008).* On January 30, 2008, three defendants, who had been extradited from the Netherlands to the

United States for their roles in a Nigerian fraud ring operating from Amsterdam, pleaded guilty to various counts of conspiracy, wire fraud, and mail fraud. According to the indictment and an earlier filed complaint,

> the defendants sent spam to thousands of potential victims, in which they falsely claimed to control millions of dollars located abroad. Attempting to conceal their identities, the defendants used a variety of aliases, phone numbers, and email addresses. In one scenario, the defendants sent emails purporting to be from an individual suffering from terminal throat cancer who needed assistance distributing approximately $55 million to charity. In exchange for a victim's help, the defendants offered to give a 20% commission to the victim or a charity of his or her choice. Subsequently, as part of the ruse, the defendants would send a variety of fraudulent documents, including a "Letter of Authority" or a "Certificate of Deposit," making it appear that the promised funds were available, and pictures of an individual claiming to suffer from throat cancer. [One defendant] allegedly telephoned victims, disguising his voice to give the impression that he was suffering from throat cancer.
>
> After obtaining their victims' trust, the defendants asked them to wire-transfer payment for a variety of advance fees, ostensibly for legal representation, taxes, and additional documentation. In return, the victims received nothing. In a variation of the scheme, if the victims said they could not afford to pay the advance fees, the defendants would send them counterfeit checks, supposedly from a cancer patient, to cover those fees. Many victims deposited the checks and then drew on them to wire-transfer the advance fees. Subsequently, when the checks did not clear, the victims suffered substantial losses.[83]

- *R. v. Anigozie et al. (Ontario, arrested November 2, 2007).* In this investigation, three Ontario residents were arrested in connection with the production and mass mailing of counterfeit checks throughout North America. The investigation was primarily focused on the "lab" where the fraudulent checks were being manufactured. Counterfeit checks and supporting documentation were allegedly being prepared in regard to fraudulent statements regarding charities, lotteries, and personal loans. Police also executed five search warrants and seized several computer systems, printers, scanners, counterfeit U.S. currency, and thousands of checks in various stages of production.[84]
- *U.S. v. Roberts (S.D. W. Va., sentenced January 2006).* In this case, the defendant was sentenced to 18 months imprisonment for his role in a scheme to distribute counterfeit checks to others. At the time of his arrest, the defendant was found to be in possession of counterfeit checks and money orders totaling more than $680,000. He later told law enforcement agents that he had met a person named "John" on the Internet, and that he had received the counterfeit checks and money orders from "John," as well as envelopes, UPS postage, and directions on how to distribute the checks to various individuals.[85]

4. Identity Theft

The following are several examples of criminal enforcement actions that have been brought since 2003 against criminals engaging in identity theft with cross-border aspects:

- *U.S. v. Hardiman (W.D.N.Y., sentenced September 12, 2007).* In this case, on September 12, 2007 a Toronto resident was sentenced to two years imprisonment for aggravated identity theft. The defendant, who trafficked in counterfeit credit cards, sold counterfeit credit cards and driver's licenses over the Internet. The counterfeit credit cards used the numbers of actual accounts issued by financial services entities, including Wachovia, Visa, and American Express. In addition, for the counterfeit drivers' licenses he produced, the defendant used actual driver's license numbers belonging to other individuals from the Canadian Provinces the licenses were purportedly issued. Both the U.S. Secret Service and the Toronto Police Service took part in the investigation.[86]

- *U.S. v. Ciocan and Pasca (W.D. Pa., indictment filed May 8, 2007).* In this case, two Romanian nationals living in Canada were indicted on federal charges of conspiracy, bank fraud, and aggravated identity theft for their roles in an identity theft scheme that involved acquiring bank customers' identifying data at ATM terminals. According to the charges in the case, the defendants allegedly

> participated in a scheme in which members of the scheme installed, on Automated Teller Machines, card readers that surreptitiously stole the account and other information from the ATM cards without the card users' knowledge or consent. Members of the conspiracy also fraudulently obtained the personal identification numbers associated with the cards. Members of the conspiracy then used the account information stolen from the ATM cards to manufacture counterfeit ATM cards. [The defendants allegedly] then traveled from city to city using the counterfeit ATM cards and the fraudulently obtained personal identification numbers to withdraw funds from various ATM machines.[87]

- *Internet-Based Identity Theft Charges (Ontario, charges laid March 2006).* In this case, Ottawa police uncovered an Internet-based identity theft scheme that targeted applicants for a job posting that was published online. Members of the scheme reportedly notified a prospective victim that he or she was a suitable candidate for the $70,000-a-year position, and asked the prospective victim to fill out an application form and to send a $20 processing fee. Once the victims submitted their personal information, the criminals used that information to apply for credit cards and identification and social insurance cards in the victims' names. Two suspects were arrested after Ottawa police executed a search warrant at a residence, seizing approximately 60 credit cards, social insurance cards and driver's licences from both Ontario and Quebec. Authorities alleged that the suspects had been operating the scam since 2002.[88]

E. Public Education and Prevention Accomplishments

Since 2003, Canadian and U.S. law enforcement authorities have continued to carry out a variety of approaches to foster improved public education and awareness about mass-marketing fraud. These include:

- **Disruption of Criminal Activity.** In late 2007, Project COLT, after learning that certain envelopes addressed to locations in the United States contained marketing fraud materials, conducted a one-month surveillance operation that led to the discovery of more than 50,000 fraudulent letters addressed to U.S. and some Canadian citizens in an attempted fraud of nearly $195 million. The letters included counterfeit checks with face amounts ranging from $2,000 to $5,000. The results of this operation provided an opportunity for the RCMP to warn the public about the seizure and the fraud schemes it had uncovered.[89]

Other kinds of efforts to disrupt criminal mass-marketing fraud operations can also provide benefits for victims. Since 1998, for example, Project COLT has recovered more than $20 million for mass-marketing fraud victims.

- **Public Advisories.** Various agencies in both countries have issued public advisories to warn the public about particular types of mass-marketing fraud activity, such as the use of counterfeit checks and money orders in fraud schemes[90] and spam falsely claiming to be sent by a law enforcement agency.[91]

- **Public Education Campaigns and Advertisements.** In 2007, the RCMP and other law enforcement agencies outside North America participated in an initiative led by the U.S. Postal Inspection Service to warn the public about the risks of counterfeit checks in fraud schemes. The educational components of this initiative included public-service advertisements on television and in print media and a website, created by the National Consumers League, with additional educational resources.[92] This initiative also involved substantial collaboration between the public and private sectors – including seven leading financial-services businesses and associations and Publishers Clearing House — in supporting and publicizing the advertising campaign.[93]

The FTC has conducted numerous public education measures and events related to mass-marketing fraud. For example, in 2006, the FTC and the U.S. Food and Drug Administration, working with government agencies in Canada and Mexico, launched a drive to stop deceptive online advertisements and sales of products misrepresented as cures or treatments for diabetes. As of October 2006, the joint campaign had included approximately 180 warning letters and other advisories sent to online outlets in the three countries.[94] Also in 2006, the FTC held a Hispanic Fraud Prevention Forum in New York City. The forum featured the announcement of new consumer education materials, and outreach partnerships with schools in New York City, as well as the results of a Hispanic Multi-Media Surf that the FTC and 60 partners in the United States and Latin America conducted.[95]

In Montreal, Canada, Project COLT initiated a public education campaign targeted specifically at potential telemarketing boiler room employees. In a series of advertisements and flyers aimed at students, Project COLT warned of the dangers of working for fraudulent businesses. Project COLT also encouraged students to report suspicious activities to law enforcement.

In 2005, the FTC, with significant contributions from DOJ, the United States Postal Inspection Service, other federal agencies, and numerous private groups, launched "On Guard Online," (www.onguardonline.gov) an interactive website that provides tips for consumers about a variety of mass-marketing frauds including identity theft, phishing, spyware, spam scams, and VoIP.

Most recently, in February 2008, the U.S. Postal Inspection Service conducted a nationwide campaign to heighten public awareness about identity theft. As part of that campaign, the Postmaster General sent out 121 million letters to every household in the United States that included an FTC brochure on identity theft.

March is Fraud Prevention Month. In Canada, during March, the Fraud Prevention Forum[96], chaired by Competition Bureau Canada, leads a concerted fraud awareness campaign. Through a wide variety of communications media and activities, the more than one hundred private and public sector organization members of the Forum deliver millions of messages to educate and alert the public about the dangers of fraud.

SECTION III: CONTINUING CHALLENGES IN MASS-MARKETING FRAUD - REFINING THE BINATIONAL ACTION PLAN

Since the 2003 Report, Canada and the United States have continued to make substantial strides in binational cooperation to combat cross-border fraud, particularly mass-marketing fraud. Thanks to their respective law enforcement authorities, additional joint task forces and strategic partnerships have been established, and investigations and prosecutions of leading offenders in mass-marketing fraud schemes successfully pursued.

At the same time, both countries' experiences with mass-marketing fraud since 2003 provide substantial evidence that continuing collaboration and sharing of scarce resources tocombat the problem is essential. On an ongoing basis, law enforcers, prosecutors, and regulators in both countries will need to decide what new steps can and should be taken to become even more effective in combating cross-border fraud schemes.

To provide a coherent framework for the steps needed to improve binational effectiveness in combating cross-border fraud, the 2003 Report presented an Action Plan that outlined key measures to strengthen existing binational capabilities to combat the most significant types of cross-border fraud that affect both countries. This Action Plan addressed strategic and operational concerns regarding investigation, prosecution, and public education and prevention of cross-border fraud schemes.

A. The Binational Action Plan for Cross-Border Fraud

The 2003 Action Plan consisted of 12 points grouped under five principal headings. This Section of the Report will discuss what steps have been taken, and still need to be taken, since the 2003 Report to carry out each of these recommendations and to offer an additional recommendation to meet the evolving threats that mass-marketing fraud poses for both countries.

1. Strategies

(1) ***Both countries should compare their respective strategies against cross-border telemarketing fraud and ensure harmonization of those strategies in addressing newer developments in telemarketing fraud.***

Since the 2003 Report, various members of national-level working groups in both countries, including this Subgroup and the Canadian Mass Marketing Fraud Strategy

Working Group, have discussed their current strategic frameworks in greater detail and identify areas where greater harmonization of those strategies would be in order. With the completion of the Mass Marketing Fraud Strategy Group's work on a national strategy, as described below, agencies in both countries should be able to coordinate their respective strategies even more closely.

(2) ***As part of that process of harmonization, both countries should also examine their existing national-level working groups that address other types of cross-border fraud issues, and where appropriate take similar steps to ensure harmonization of national strategies in addressing those types of fraud.***

Since the 2003 Report, in 2005 Canadian law enforcement partners established the National Mass Marketing Fraud Strategy Working Group. This working group, which drew on the expertise and advice of numerous Canadian and U.S. law enforcement agencies, identified a "four pillar" strategy for controlling, dismantling and neutralizing the criminal activities of mass marketing fraud operations in Canada and internationally. The four pillars of this strategy are: (1) more vigorous law enforcement; (2) increasing public awareness and reporting; (3) creating tougher sanctions and more targeted legislation; and (4) increased information sharing and cooperation.[97] The adoption and full implementation of this strategy will necessarily require continued and close coordination between Canada and the United States on strategic and tactical approaches to combating mass-marketing fraud of all types.

2. Operational Efforts

(3) ***Agencies that are members of existing interagency telemarketing fraud task forces should reaffirm their commitment to participation in those task forces, and consider inclusion of new agencies where appropriate to obtain additional investigative resources against cross-border fraud.***

Since the 2003 Report, as described earlier, there are now six active Canadian-based task forces and strategic partnerships directed at mass-marketing fraud. Although some agencies no longer participate in certain task forces and partnerships, the operations of the task forces and partnerships since 2003 provide substantial and concrete evidence that they continue to make very substantial contributions to the fight against cross-border mass-marketing fraud. Continuation of those efforts is dependent on key participants in those task forces and partnerships continuing their membership and, as appropriate, attracting additional law enforcement or regulatory members at all levels of law enforcement to enhance their capabilities as mass-marketing fraud schemes continue to evolve.

(4) ***In investigating and preparing to prosecute cases against particular cross-border fraud schemes for prosecution, police, law enforcement agents, and prosecutors should explore all avenues for seizing and forfeiting proceeds of the crimes traceable to those schemes and returning as much money as possible in restitution to victims of the schemes.***

Since the 2003 Report, law enforcement authorities in both countries have shown greater interest in making use of their respective legal procedures for tracing, seizing, and forfeiting the proceeds of major mass-marketing fraud schemes. While the opportunities and capabilities for seizing and forfeiting mass-marketing fraud proceeds will necessarily vary from case to case, law enforcement and prosecutive agencies should continue to incorporate consideration of seizure and forfeiture into their strategic planning of particular cases, and use all available legal authority as appropriate in those cases.

(5) ***In investigating cross-border fraud cases, prosecutive offices in both countries should continue to examine the speed with which mutual legal assistance requests are processed and carried out, and to look for ways of expediting the processing of such requests.***

Since the 2003 Report, the Cross Border Crime Forum has taken up this issue directly and assigned it to the Prosecutions Subgroup for further action. That Subgroup in turn has been systematically examining the problems associated with timely assistance under the Canada-U.S. Mutual Legal Assistance Treaty (MLAT) and extradition treaty.

(6) ***Prosecutors and civil enforcement agencies in both countries should consider whether to use "sweeps" - a series of coordinated enforcement actions against similar types of criminal or fraudulent activities – in selected categories of cross-border fraud cases.***

Since the 2003 Report, law enforcement authorities in both countries have spearheaded two major multinational sweeps directed at specific categories of mass-marketing fraud. First, in the U.S. Attorney General, together with Canadian and other law enforcement officials, announced "Operation Roaming Charge." This operation, which the U.S. Attorney General and other U.S. and Canadian law enforcement officials announced on October 5, 2004, was the most extensive multinational enforcement operation ever directed at domestic and international telemarketing fraud operations. The nine-month operation involved more than 100 separate investigations that led to the discovery of more than five million victims, who suffered losses totaling more than $1 billion. It resulted in the arrest of more than 100 individuals in the United States, and an additional 35 arrests in other countries; the execution of more than 190 U.S. and Canadian search warrants; the conviction of 70 individuals by the date of the operation's announcement; and the filing by state attorneys general of 279 criminal, civil and regulatory actions against illegal telemarketing operations.[98]

More recently, on May 23, 2006, the U.S. Attorney General and other law enforcement officials announced the results of Operation Global Con. This operation, which ran for 15 months in 2005 and 2006, was the largest and most far-reaching multinational enforcement operation ever directed at mass-marketing fraud schemes. In this operation, 96 separate U.S. investigations in this operation led to the discovery of more than 2.8 million victims, who suffered losses totaling more than $1 billion. It resulted in the arrest of 139 individuals in the United States, and an additional 426 arrests in Canada, Costa Rica, the Netherlands, and Spain; the execution of 447 search warrants in those five countries; 61 convictions as of the date of the announcement; and the filing of 20 civil actions by the FTC against 140 defendants.[99]

Sweeps such as Roaming Charge and Global Con offer significant benefits to law enforcement in several respects. Apart from the immediate opportunities that they provide for public education messages, these operations also demonstrate the value of sustained long-term planning, information-sharing, and coordination among law enforcement agencies in multiple countries. If they are to have the maximum impact on international mass-marketing fraud, law enforcement agencies will need to pool their intelligence and enforcement resources efficiently to identify and pursue the most significant mass-marketing fraud operations and their ringleaders, while generating additional valuable criminal intelligence that benefits governments in their enforcement and education efforts. As circumstances permit, investigative and prosecutive agencies in both countries should consider organizing and conducting other enforcement sweeps against mass-marketing fraud schemes, and to engage other countries as appropriate in those sweeps, to increase the impact of their efforts.

(7) ***Law enforcement agents and prosecutors in both countries should explore how to make more effective use of videoconferencing technology to obtain needed testimony from witnesses in the United States.***

Since the 2003 Report, both countries have found that videoconferencing continues to have the same potential values and limitations (e.g., logistical complexities and cost) for testimony in Canadian proceedings. U.S. agencies should therefore be prepared to respond when needed to Canadian requests for assistance with remote testimony from U.S. residents, and to coordinate with each other as appropriate to distribute the potential burden of providing such support on a case-by-case basis.

3. Information Sharing

(8) ***Both countries should take steps to facilitate the prompt sharing, both at national levels and among existing and future interagency task forces, of public information about enforcement actions against cross-border fraud schemes that law enforcement, prosecutive, and regulatory agencies in either country have taken, including information about the impact of those schemes on individuals and businesses.***

Since the 2003 Report, both countries have made only limited progress towards this goal. While Canada and the United States have individually made more information available to the general public about their respective enforcement efforts against mass-marketing fraud, they need to develop more systematic approaches and mechanisms to share such information on a timely basis among law enforcement agencies in both countries and in other countries. Both countries have initiated the process of developing such approaches and mechanisms, and have identified several promising practices for that purpose.

(9) ***Both countries should coordinate their efforts to contact other countries whose citizens are being targeted in cross-border fraud schemes, to share information and training opportunities with appropriate government agencies in those countries, and to take specific steps toward expanded cooperation and coordination with those countries in investigating and prosecuting such schemes.***

Since the 2003 Report, both countries have taken several steps to coordinate with several other countries, such as Australia, New Zealand, and the United Kingdom. As this chapter has shown, the effects of cross-border fraud schemes increasingly are being felt beyond North

America. Residents of the United Kingdom, Australia, and New Zealand are now being targeted, as residents of Canada and the United States have been. Law enforcement agencies in both countries should share information about which points of contacts in other countries would be the most suitable for coordinated outreach on cross-border fraud issues, and engage in coordinated outreach to exchange information about fraud issues and explore ideas for further information-sharing, training, and other cooperative ventures.

4. Coordination Between Public and Private Sectors

(10) ***Both countries should coordinate their efforts to consult with entities in the financial services and electronic payments industries about specific measures to reduce the use of particular payments mechanisms by cross-border fraud schemes.***

Since the 2003 Report, various agencies in both countries have taken the initiative to consult with private-sector financial entities about the exploitation of specific payments mechanisms, such as money transfer businesses and electronic funds transfers. To date, however, both countries have not yet carried out this recommendation for binational coordination on such consultations. Governments in both countries would benefit from coordinating their efforts in this regard, particularly with reference to the abuse of payment mechanisms such as money transfer businesses and payment processors and the growing use of counterfeit checks in mass-marketing schemes.

5. Training

(11) ***Both countries should plan to have at least one conference each year at which investigators and prosecutors can exchange information about current trends and developments in cross-border fraud and receive training about investigative techniques and substantive and procedural laws that have proven effective against major fraud schemes.***

Since the 2003 Report, both countries have continued to have annual conferences to discuss trends and developments in cross-border fraud and provide training on legal and investigative approaches to such cases. Most recently, in February 2008, the Alberta Partnership Against Cross Border Fraud , in partnership with the National Mass Marketing Fraud Strategy Working Group in Canada and the Canadian Anti-Fraud Call Center (PhoneBusters) held an International Investigators' Skills Development Workshop in Banff, Alberta. The workshop, which featured speakers from numerous Canadian, U.S., and other law enforcement agencies, was attended by more than 200 participants. In addition, the U.S. Department of Justice's National Advocacy Center, on roughly an annual basis, has conducted training seminars on international white-collar crime that has been available to non-U.S. law enforcement representatives. Because participants in these conferences and seminars uniformly find that they have appreciable value for investigators and prosecutors, both countries should continue the practice of annual conferences and explore additional opportunities to share information on mass-marketing fraud trends and training.

(12) ***Both countries should also explore the use of videoconferencing for joint binational or multinational training on specific fraud-related topics.***

Both countries, as outlined in the 2003 report, have made use of videoconferencing for training purposes. Both the United States and Canada are willing to continue to use videoconferencing for these purposes in the future.

B. Further Recommendation

(13) Both countries should enhance their capabilities to assemble criminal intelligence on emerging trends in mass-marketing fraud and to share that intelligence, consistent with applicable legal requirements, with each other and with additional countries' law enforcement agencies.

As certain aspects of international mass-marketing fraud – among others, the continuing growth and expansion of Nigerian-led criminal groups' engagement in a wide variety of mass-marketing schemes – become apparent to law enforcement agencies, law enforcement in both countries need to move promptly in identifying what types of criminal intelligence will be most useful to them in responding to those trends, and how that intelligence can best be amassed, analyzed, and disseminated in useful forms to other interested law enforcement and regulatory agencies. While each country must be sensitive to all applicable domestic legal constraints on information-gathering and -sharing, law enforcement authorities must work within those constraints to improve their effectiveness in combating the dominant and emerging strains of mass-marketing fraud. Recent experience has shown, in a number of mass-marketing fraud investigations and prosecutions, that mass-marketing fraud enforcement depends on enhancing multinational, not merely binational, cooperation.

In their first ten years of formal binational cooperation, Canada and the United States have laid a firm foundation – through information-sharing, disruption of criminal activity, public education and prevention, and enforcement – to combat all forms of mass-marketing fraud more effectively than ever before. Maintaining and strengthening that foundation will be essential to both countries' responses to the evolving threat that mass-marketing fraud continues to pose to consumers, commercial entities, and governments alike.

End Notes

[1] *See* UNITED STATES -CANADA WORKING GROUP, UNITED STATES -CANADA COOPERATION AGAINST CROSS-BORDER TELEMARKETING FRAUD (November 1997) (hereinafter 1997 Report), *copy available at* http://strategis.ic.gc.ca/pics/ct/
reporte.pdf.

[2] *See, e.g., id.* at 7, 20-22, 25, 28, 29.

[3] Canadian authorities refer to "West African Fraud".

[4] 2006 CANADA/US ORGANIZED CRIME THREAT ASSESSMENT, *available at* http://www.rcmp-grc.gc.ca/organizedcrime/octa_e.htm.

[5] *Id.*

[6] *See* National Consumers League, 2006 Top 10 Telemarketing Scam Trends from NCL's Fraud Center, January – December 2006 [hereinafter NCL 2006 TELEMARKETING TRENDS], *available at* http://fraud.org/stats/2006/telemarketing.pdf.

[7] *See id.*

[8] *See* Phonebusters, Monthly Summary Report (2007), *available a*http://www.phonebusters.com/english/documents/Yearly2007_000.pdf.

[9] *See* p. 12 *infra*.

[10] *See* 2006 CANADA/US ORGANIZED CRIME THREAT ASSESSMENT, *supra* note 3.

[11] Other organized crime groups extort payments from telemarketing fraud operators.

[12] Within Canada, cross-border business-to-business schemes appear to be especially prevalent in the Montreal area. Law enforcement authorities estimate that there are approximately 50 known business-to-business operations in Montreal, each typically employing between 10 and 30 people. Some business-to-business operations, however, have been substantially larger. In October 2007, law enforcement authorities in Montreal raided one large "business-to-business" operation that occupied several floors of a single office building and employed approximately 100 "pitchers" (i.e., employees who called prospective victims) to "pitch" business directories and first-aid kits. The operation reportedly targeted small and medium-sized busineses in Canada, the United States, and Europe. That raid resulted in more than 120 arrests. *See* Jan Ravensbergen, *Alleged fraud ring busted*, Montreal Gazette, October 9, 2007, *available at* http://www.canada.com.

[13] *See* Paul Cherry, *Bogus telemarketing head guilty of violating competition laws*, Montreal Gazette, February 26, 2008, *available at* http://www.canada.com/montrealgazette/news/story.html?id=bd5d6d66-9ece-49a1-a09d-e629ca 7584eb&k=76148.

[14] Federal Communications Comm'n, IP-Enabled Services, *available at* http://www.fcc.gov/voip/.

[15] *See* NCL 2006 TELEMARKETING TRENDS, *supra* note 6.

[16] *See* FEDERAL TRADE COMM'N, CONSUMER FRAUD AND IDENTITY THEFT COMPLAINT DATA: JANUARY-DECEMBER 2007 at (February 2008) [hereinafter FTC 2007 COMPLAINT DATA], *available at* http://www.ftc.gov/opa/2008/02/fraud.pdf.

[17] The FTC stated that "Median is the middle number in a set of numbers so that half the numbers have values that are greater than the median and half have values that are less. Calculation of the median excludes complaints with amount paid reported as $0." *Id.* at 10.

[18] *Id.*

[19] *See id.* at 11.

[20] INTERNET CRIME COMPLAINT CENTER, INTERNET CRIME REPORT: JANUARY 1, 2006 DECEMBER 31, 2006 at 3 (2007), *available at* http://www.ic3.gov/media/annualreport/2006_IC3Report.pdf.

[21] *See* National Consumers League, 2006 Top 10 Internet Scam Trends from NCL's Fraud Center, January – December 2006, *available at* http://fraud.org/stats/2006/internet.pdf.

[22] *Id.*

[23] *See id.*

[24] *See id.*

[25] *See* PhoneBusters, Monthly Summary Report, *supra* note 8.

[26] *See id.*

[27] *See* FEDERAL TRADE COMM'N, CONSUMER FRAUD AND IDENTITY THEFT COMPLAINT DATA: JANUARY - DECEMBER 2007 at 4 (February 2008).

[28] 2006 CANADA/US ORGANIZED CRIME THREAT ASSESSMENT, *supra* note 4.

[29] *See* ANTI-PHISHING WORKING GROUP, PHISHING ATTACK TRENDS REPORT: JANUARY, 2004 at 1, 3 (2004) [hereinafter APWG JANUARY 2004 TRENDS REPORT], *available at* http://www.antiphishing.org/reports/APWG.Phishing.Attack.Report.Jan2004.pdf.

[30] *See* ANTI-PHISHING WORKING GROUP, PHISHING ACTIVITY TRENDS: REPORT FOR THE MONTH OF NOVEMBER, 2007 at 1 (2008) [hereinafter APWG NOVEMBER 2007 TRENDS REPORT], *available at* http://www.antiphishing.org/reports/apwg_report_nov_2007.pdf.

[31] *See id.* at 6.

[32] *See* APWG JANUARY 2004 TRENDS REPORT a, *supra* note 29, at 1.

[33] *See* APWG NOVEMBER 2007 TRENDS REPORT, *supra* note 30, at 1, 5.

[34] *See id.* at 5.

[35] *Id.* at 3.

[36] *Id.*

[37] *See* APWG JANUARY 2004 TRENDS REPORT, *supra* note 29, at 3.

[38] *Id.* at 4.

[39] A URL is the online address of a website, document, or other resource on the World Wide Web. A URL address consists of two parts: (1) a protocol identifier (e.g., http or ftp) that indicates what Internet protocol to use in accessing that address; and (2) a resource name that specifies the Internet protocol (IP) address or domain name where the resource is located. *See* Webopedia, http://www.webopedia.com.

[40] *See* APWG NOVEMBER 2007 TRENDS REPORT , *supra* note 30 at 7.

[41] *See id.* at 8.

[42] *Id.* at 7.

[43] *Id.* at 8.

[44] *See* SOPHOS, SECURITY THREAT REPORT at 2 (2008), *available at* http://www.sophos.com/security/whitepapers/sophos-security-report-2008.

[45] *See, e.g.,* CIBC, E-mail Fraud (Phishing), *available at* http://www.cibc.com/ca/legal/phishing-info.html; MBNA Canada, Fraud Reporting & Prevention, available at http://www.mbna.ca/fraud_protect.html; RBC, Email and Website Fraud (Phishing), *available at* http://www.rbc.com/security/bulletinPhishing.html.

[46] *See, e.g.*, BINATIONAL WORKING GROUP ON CROSS-BORDER MASS-MARKETING FRAUD, SPECIAL REPORT ON PHISHING (October 2006), available at http://www.usdoj.gov/opa/report_on_phishing.pdf;

[47] *See, e.g.*, *Beware phishing scam, TD Canada Trust warns customers*, CBC News, Jul 31, 2007, *available at* http://www.cbc.ca/technology/story/2007/07/31/tech-td-phishing.html; U.S. Dep't of Justice, Alert About Hoax Emails (January 30, 2008), *available at* http://www.usdoj.gov/hoaxemail.htm.

[48] *See, e.g.*, PRESIDENT'S IDENTITY THEFT TASK FORCE, COMBATING IDENTITY THEFT: A STRATEGIC PLAN at 14-18 (April 2007), available at http://www.idtheft.gov; Public Safety Canada, Advice for consumers: Identity theft, http://www.publicsafety.gc.ca/prg/le/bs/consumers-en.asp.

[49] *See, e.g.*, *Police ask for help in card skimming case*, Owen Sound Sun-Times, January 22, 2008, *available at* http://www.owensoundsuntimes.com/ArticleDisplay.aspx?e=869831&auth=Keith+Gilbert%2FS un+Media; *Regina bank customers hit by debit-card skimmers*, CBC News, April 2, 2007, *available at* http://www.cbc.ca/canada/saskatchewan/story/2007/04/02/regina-skimmers.html.

[50] Royal Canadian Mounted Police, Identity Theft, *available at* http://www.rcmp-grc.gc.ca/scams/identity_theft_e.htm.

[51] *See, e.g.*, Kelly Martin, *Stop the bots*, SecurityFocus, April 18, 2006, *available at* http://www.securityfocus.com/columnists/398/1.

[52] *See* SANS Institute, Press Release (January 14, 2008), *available at* http://www.sans.org/press/top10menaces08.php.

[53] Department of Justice Canada, Press Release (November 21, 2007), *available at* http://www.justice.gc.ca/en/news/nr/2007/doc_32178.html.

[54] Pub. L. No. 109-455, 120 Stat. 3372 (December 22, 2006), *available at* http://www.ftc.gov/ogc/FTC_Act_IncorporatingUS_SAFE_WEB_Act.pdf

[55] *See* Congressional Research Service, Summary of S. 1608, *available at* http://thomas.loc.gov/cgi-bin/bdquery/z?d109:SN01608:@@@D&summ2=m&.

[56] *See* PRESIDENT'S IDENTITY THEFT TASK FORCE, COMBATING IDENTITY THEFT: A STRATEGIC PLAN (2008), *available at* http://www.idtheft.gov.

[57] 18 U.S.C. 1028(a)(7).

[58] 18 U.S.C. 1028A.

[59] 18 U.S.C. 1030.

[60] 18 U.S.C. 1030(a)(7).

[61] *See* PRESIDENT'S IDENTITY THEFT TASK FORCE, *supra* note 56, at 7, 9.

[62] The Canadian Anti-Fraud Call Centre, PhoneBusters, About Us, *available at* http://www.phonebusters.com/english/aboutus.html.

[63] *See* RECOL, *available at* https://www.recol.ca/intro.aspx?lang=en.

[64] Consumer Measures Committee, Cooperative Enforcement - Working Group, *available at* http://cmcweb.ca/epic/site/cmc-cmc.nsf/en/fe00030e.html.

[65] *See* Service Alberta, Press Release, *available at* http://www.servicealberta.gov.ab.ca/987.cfm.

[66] *See* 2007 FTC COMPLAINT DATA, *supra* note 16, at 2.

[67] *See* Internet Crime Complaint Center, *available at* http://www.ic3.gov/.

[68] *See* National Cyber-Forensics and Training Alliance, *available at* http://www.ncfta.net/default2.asp.

[69] U.S. Attorney's Office, Central District of California, Press Release (December 19, 2007), *available at* http://www.usdoj.gov/usao/cac/pressroom/pr2007/163.html.

[70] *See id.*

[71] *See* Royal Canadian Mounted Police, "C" Division, Press Release (January 4, 2008), *available at* http://www.rcmp-grc.gc.ca/qc/comm/2008/01/080104_e.htm.

[72] FBI, Press Release (November 6, 2007), *available at* http://losangeles.fbi.gov/pressrel/2007/la110607a.htm.

[73] *See* FTC, Press Release (November 19, 2007), *available at* http://www.ftc.gov/opa/2007/11/cashcorner.shtm.

[74] *See id.*

[75] *See* U.S. Attorney's Office, Southern District of Illinois, Press Release (October 29, 2007), *available at* http://www.usdoj.gov/usao/ils/press/2007/Oct/10292007_Porcelli_press%20release.htm.

[76] *See* Royal Canadian Mounted Police, "C" Division, Press Release (October 9, 2007), *available at* http://www.rcmp-grc.gc.ca/qc/comm/archives/2007/10/071009_e.htm.

[77] *See* U.S. Attorney's Office, Southern District of Illinois,, Press Release (June 20, 2007), *available at* http://www.usdoj.gov/usao/ils/press/2007/Jun/06202007_Kimoto%20press%20release.htm.

[78] *See* Final Monetary Judgment As To Defendants Kyle Kimoto and Assail, Inc., FTC v. Assail, Civil Action No. W-03-CA-007 (W.D. Tex., September 24, 2004), *available at* http://www.ftc.gov/os/caselist/assail/050124kimoto.pdf.

[79] *See* U.S. Attorney's Office, Western District of New York, Press Release (April 2, 2007), *available at* http://www.usdoj.gov/usao/nyw/press/press_releases/BROWNANDLOVEPRESS.pdf.

[80] *See* U.S. Attorney's Office, District of Oregon, Press Release (February 25, 2007), *available at* http://portland.fbi.gov/dojpressrel/2007/investmentscheme022507.htm; U.S. Attorney's Office, District of

Oregon, Press Release (October 24, 2006), *available at* http://portland.fbi.gov/dojpressrel/2006/investmentfrau102406.htm.

[81] *See* U.S. Attorney's Office, Southern District of Florida, Press Release (May 8, 2006), *available at* http://miami.fbi.gov/dojpressrel/pressrel06/mm050806.htm.

[82] *See* FBI, Busted for Katrina Fraud (October 21, 2005), *available at* http://www.fbi.gov/page2/oct05/katrinaescam102105.htm.

[83] *See* U.S. Attorney's Office, Eastern District of New York, Press Release (January 30, 2008), *available at* http://www.usdoj.gov/usao/nye/pr/2008/2008jan30.html.

[84] *See* Ontario Provincial Police, Press Release (November 2, 2007).

[85] *See* U.S. Attorney's Office, Southern District of West Virginia, Press Release (January 11, 2006), *available at* http://www.usdoj.gov/usao.wvs/press_releases/2006/jan06/011106.html.

[86] *See* U.S. Attorney's Office, Western District of New York, Press Release (September 12, 2007), *available at* http://www.usdoj.gov/usao/nyw/press/press_releases/HardimanSentencing.pdf.

[87] U.S. Attorney's Office, Western District of Pennsylvania, Press Release (October 9, 2007), *available at* http://pittsburgh.fbi.gov/dojpressrel/2007/identitytheft050907.htm.

[88] *See Two charged in Internet-based identity theft scam*, ctv.ca, March 9, 2006, *available at* http://www.ctv.ca/servlet/ArticleNews/story/CTVNews/20060308/idtheft_scam_060308?s_nam e=&no_ads=.

[89] *See* RCMP, "C" Division, Press Release (December 18, 2007), *available at* http://www.rcmp-grc.gc.ca/qc/comm/archives/2007/12/071218_e.htm.

[90] *See* Public Safety and Emergency Preparedness Canada and U.S. Dep't of Justice, Public Advisory: Special Report on Counterfeit Checks and Money Orders, *available at* http://www.usdoj.gov/opa/public_advisory_counterfeit.pdf.

[91] *See, e.g.,* U.S. Secret Service, FRAUDULENT SPAM E-MAIL CLAIMING TO BE FROM THE U.S. SECRET SERVICE (January 26, 2007), *available at* http://www.secretservice.gov/fraud_email_advisory.shtml.

[92] *See* fakechecks.org, *available at* http://www.fakechecks.org/.

[93] *See* fakechecks.org, About Us, *available at* http://www.fakechecks.org/links.html.

[94] *See* Food and Drug Administration, Press Release (October 19, 2006), *available at* http://www.fda.gov/bbs/topics/NEWS/2006/NEW01494.html.

[95] *See* FTC, Press Release (September 27, 2006), *available at* http://www.ftc.gov/opa/2006/09/nyworkshop.shtm.

[96] *See* 2008 Fraud Prevention Month Campaign and Fraud Prevention Forum membership *available at* http://www.competitionbureau.gc.ca/epic/site/cb-bc.nsf/en/h_00122e.html

[97] *See* JESSE CALE, JOHN WINTERDYK, NIKKI THOMPSON & PATRICK NEAL, TOWARDS A NATIONAL STRATEGY AGAINST MASS MARKETING FRAUD IN CANADA (2007), *available at* http://www.bpcpa.ca/images/content/publications/nmmf%20strategy%20report2007.pdf.

[98] *See* U.S. Dep't of Justice, Press Release (October 5, 2004), *available at* http://www.usdoj.gov/opa/pr/2004/October/04_crm_680.htm.

[99] *See* U.S. Dep't of Justice, Press Release (May 23, 2006), *available at* http://www.usdoj.gov/opa/pr/2006/May/06_crm_321.html.

INDEX

A

B

C

D

E

F

G

H

I

N

O

P

Q

R